W9-BER-742

Presented to

_____

By

_____

On the Occasion of

_____

Date

_____

CREATED FOR A PURPOSE

A MESSAGE OF HOPE FOR THE WOMAN STRUGGLING WITH ISSUES OF SELF-ESTEEM

Darlene Sala

BARBOUR
PUBLISHING, INC.
Uhrichsville, Ohio

CREATED
FOR A
PURPOSE

ISBN 1-57748-588-2

Published by Barbour Publishing, Inc., P.O. Box 719,
Uhrichsville, OH 44683 http://www.barbourbooks.com

Member of the
Evangelical Christian
Publishers Association

Printed in the United States of America.

ACKNOWLEDGMENTS

Each book is really the product of many people, because all those who touch the life of an author influence his or her work. I give special thanks, however, to my husband, Harold, and my three children—Bonnie, Steven, and Nancy—who have inspired me and edited this manuscript multiple times.

A big thanks to Susan Johnson, Senior Editor at Barbour Publishing, for seeing potential in the original manuscript. Thank you, Toni Sorter, for your editorial skills in helping me make sure that "what I said is what I meant." Ellyn Sanna, you remind me of an assistant in the delivery room, encouraging, smoothing the rough places, and helping me give birth to ideas and thoughts in such a way that the book is still "my baby."

Thank you, too, to the staff of Guidelines, for your input in areas where I lacked experience. Special appreciation to Kathy for sharing her story so openly. And, finally, thank you to my parents for laying the foundation that helps me know I was "created for a purpose."

*Dedicated to
four significant women in my life—
my mom, my two daughters,
and my daughter-in-law—
women who have cheered me on
to press toward the goal of taking hold of
"that for which Christ Jesus took hold of me"*
PHILIPPIANS 3:12

CONTENTS

PREFACE

I read all the letters that pour into Guidelines International Ministries. It's a great job! Who wouldn't enjoy hearing from people whose lives have been changed by hearing God's Word? They have acted on it in faith, and now they are seeing it at work in their lives. Day after day, my heart is lifted by these stories of faith and victory. I am excited and encouraged to read of lives made whole that once were shattered.

But many of the letters we receive are not enjoyable to read. Some are filled with heartache; some come from women who are enduring more problems than anyone should have to deal with in one lifetime. These women have fallen into a pit so deep that they can no longer even see the tiny sunlit circle above them. Can't you just feel the anguish in this woman's letter?

My husband left me for another man's wife and married her. We were married for twenty-nine and one-half years. My children—five of them—and I had no idea he felt the way he did. Three months before he asked me for a divorce, I got a card in the mail from him, signed, "To the best wife in the whole world—all my love forever." My whole life has changed—upside down and inside out. Pain—I have never felt so much pain. I almost killed myself. I wish I could close my eyes and wake up and find this is all a bad dream.

Another woman was in such despair that she was in serious danger of taking her own life. Her letter was a cry for help that could not be ignored.

I just heard your five-minute talk on suicide. I have spent most of the night weighing the pros and cons of suicide. The depression just won't leave. I can't stand it any longer. Medicine doesn't help. All I do is cry. Where is God? Please send the book you mentioned. I only hope I'll still be here when it comes.

Not all the letters that come to us are this dramatic, but they all touch my heart. Some are from mothers so burdened with caring for their little ones and trying to make ends meet that they feel their lives count for nothing. They have no time for anything but their daily struggle for survival, and that struggle has buried their individuality. Not only do they fail to see God's presence in their lives, they also fail to appreciate their own worth in God's eyes.

It is the middle of the night, and here I am writing to you. I am supposed to be trusting in Jesus. But today I look to Him but I find no comfort. What is bothering me is me—who am I? I am only nineteen. My mother and father are gone. I am the last of nine children. I have two children I love, and they're all I have to live for. Please write me back.

We all know women who are suffering in one way or another. Husbands leave; unrelenting despair takes hold of lives; and God seems far away. Some suffering women will survive and rebuild their lives. Others will only fall deeper and deeper into the pit.

Monica Lewinsky was an attractive young woman with great potential and talents. And yet she chose to waste all that potential by becoming involved with a married man, the president of the United States, tangling herself in one of the worst scandals of modern times. In an interview with Barbara Walters, Monica was asked, "Where was your self-esteem?" Her reply? "I don't have the feeling of self-worth that a woman should have, and that's hard for me, and I think that's been a center of a lot of my mistakes and a lot of my pain." Monica's mistakes have been more obvious to the entire world than some other woman's may have been—but the pain and lack of self-esteem in her heart is very similar to what many women face.

What makes one woman capable of turning her life around while another cannot? My experience has been that what a woman believes about herself makes a difference in how she deals with difficulty. I'm not talking here about thinking positively. Positive thinking works fine if the situation is somewhat under your control. If you lose your job, you can find another. If your marriage has gone stale, there are ways to renew it. But what about those situations that you are truly helpless to change? I believe that if you see yourself as God sees you—if you have a good sense of self-esteem—you will somehow be able to cope with almost anything, because you will find that God's grace is indeed sufficient for you.

Most women, however, tend to get their sense of self-esteem from three sources: their accomplishments, their appearance, and from their relationships. Unfortunately, as we'll discuss in chapter 5, all of these are susceptible to change. No matter how talented we are, some of our efforts will fail; sickness, accidents, and, most commonly, time itself will touch our looks; and one way or other, even the best and most loving relationship has an end in this world.

There is good news, though. As women, we do not need to be dependent on any of these three things for our self-esteem. Instead, we can rely on our value in God's eyes—and that will never change. "The king's daughter is all glorious within," says Psalm 45:13 (KJV). Through Jesus Christ, we can become King's daughters—and we will be truly glorious in God's eyes, through the transforming power of His Son.

Steve Arterburn, chairman and CEO of New Life Treatment Centers, says that the goal of secular counseling is to make you feel *good* about yourself, but the goal of biblical counseling is to make you feel *right* about yourself. That is also the goal of this book. It is written specifically for women because in my experience women struggle more with the issue of self-esteem than men do. The most heartbreaking letters we receive come from women.

This is not to say that men develop self-esteem more easily than women just because they are men. From childhood, men are conditioned to act, not feel. We know that in truth they *do* feel, but what we see are their actions, not their pain. To a man, emotional pain is something to be swallowed down and denied. Sometimes even their wives never suspect that they are suffering. Achievement of any kind brings self-esteem, and if there is one thing men are taught today, it's to achieve in the world, to feed their families, and prove their worth in their day-to-day lives—through their actions, not their feelings.

Women, on the other hand, are conditioned to care for others, to be supportive, and to develop their self-esteem on the basis of their relationships with others. The most successful career woman in the city is still expected to dress her children in clean clothing, keep her husband fed and cared for, get along with everyone in the office or church, and contribute to the lives of others in her "spare time." If she is capable of doing all this with grace, good humor, and love, others will respect her, and their respect will build her self-esteem.

Can you see how this leaves women with the short end of the stick? A man is allowed more latitude in his personal and professional life. He is allowed to be a real stinker, personally, as long as he produces. If he achieves, he builds his self-esteem. Women, on the other hand, must be pleasant and nurturing while they achieve. Their success depends more on their personality, on how others see them. If a woman's self-esteem depends on how others see her, then it is not in her own control. It's one thing to be able to do a job well and an entirely different thing to do a job well and have people at the office appreciate you.

You may be struggling today with an incorrect sense of your own worth. It may manifest itself as an eating disorder, compulsive spending, depression, fearfulness, obsession with your appearance, or any one of a number of other ways. You may be disappointed when I don't deal individually with those painful problems. While my heart goes out to you, covering all of those problems would fill a very large book![1]

Moreover, it is my experience that many of these issues are either the symptoms or the results of poor self-esteem, not the root cause. While the symptoms are serious enough on their own, we must deal with their cause, not just slap on a bandage and ignore the infection. If we did that, the problem would just break out in a different set of symptoms.

If you are struggling with these issues, I would like to put my arms around you and whisper that God loves you—that you are valuable to

Him and He made you because He wants to create eternal beauty through all that you are experiencing.

What I hope to give you in this book is a basis—a foundation—for understanding your worth, no matter what your personality, life story, talents, or limitations. You may need additional help or counseling to deal with a specific issue, but in order to build a lasting sense of your own worth, first you need a good foundation, one based not on what you *do* but who you *are*. No, you may not feel good about yourself every day, but if you see yourself as God sees you, you can feel *right* about yourself every day. You'll know you are a person of worth to God and that He is working in your life to bring you abundant life through His Son—and glory to Himself.

Sometimes, though, we all get tired and frustrated. Mary Hollingworth's book addresses these feelings.

> Do you ever get tired of being a woman? Do you sometimes wish you could just be somebody else for a few days?
> When you see mountains of

laundry, a list of errands as long as your arm, and a stack of paperwork that needed attention yesterday, would you just like to scream and run out the door? "Here, honey, you be the woman this week. Bye!"

. . .[But] wouldn't you miss just being you—an amazing, creative, needed, capable, blessed, and loved woman?

Celebrate! You are God's extended feminine presence in this world. Without you, the world would have an incomplete picture of God. You are woman. . .God's woman.[2]

You are God's woman—and He has a purpose for you, a purpose that will bring Him glory. That's what we'll be talking about in this book.

So let's get started.

*I have come that they may have life,
and have it to the full.*
JOHN 10:10

Jesus doesn't want you to have a pinched, skinny little life, a life that's constricted by doubts and fears about your own worth. No, He wants you to have a life that's full and rich. That's what this Bible verse from the Gospel of John is saying: Jesus wants you to really *live*. The King James Version of the Bible calls the same concept "abundant" life. In the Gospel of Luke, Jesus says that "a good measure, pressed down, shaken together and running over, will be poured into your lap" (6:38).

This isn't the way the world pictures the Christian life. People who don't know Christ tend to think that the life He offers is one that's full of legalistic rules and restrictions. But instead, Jesus loves you so much that He came to earth and died—so that through Him, you could have a real life, a full life—forever.

And He came for women, just as much as He did for men. If you read through the Gospels, you'll notice how many of the stories have to do with women. This is all the more unusual when you think that Jesus lived in a time and culture when women were truly considered second-class citizens. And yet Jesus never failed to reach out with love and compassion and healing to every woman He met. He came to earth especially for everyone whom the world ignores, for everyone who suffers under a heavy load, for everyone who feels worthless and wounded.

Jesus is reaching out to you today with the same compassionate love. He wants to heal your wounded self-esteem. You are precious to Him. When you give your identity to Him, He will give you back more than you can ever imagine. He wants to free you from all your doubts about your own worth. He wants you to live life to its full.

GOING FURTHER. . .

1. What do you think is the difference between "feeling *good* about yourself" and "feeling *right* about yourself"?

2. List some of the outward forms that poor self-esteem can take.

3. When you look at your own life, what symptoms of poor self-esteem do you see?

4. Whenever you look in the mirror this week, whisper to yourself, "I am precious to Jesus."

*S*ometimes, God, I feel as though I can't do anything right. I try so hard—but I never can do all the things I feel I should. Something's always left undone—or else it's done, but not very well! I get so frustrated and discouraged sometimes that I just want to give up. Times like these, I don't like myself very much.

Dear God, help me to turn to You whenever I feel like this. Remind me that I can feel right about myself even on the days when I don't feel good about myself. Thank You for loving me so much that You sent Jesus. Thank You for the full, abundant life You offer me.

AMEN

CHAPTER 1

SELF-ESTEEM

Our Definition and God's Definition

Self-esteem is certainly a familiar phrase these days, but its meaning seems to change, depending on who is leading the discussion. Countless books and magazine articles have been written about it from various viewpoints. Businesses hold expensive seminars to develop self-esteem in their employees. School systems devise programs to promote self-esteem in both students and teachers. And the business of plastic surgery mushrooms as people set out on their personal quests for self-esteem, hoping that a perfect nose makes a perfect person.

In the 1950s, television brought "perfect" women right into our homes so we could compare ourselves to them and see how far short we fell. What mother had the patience of June Cleaver? What young wife had the charm of Mary Tyler Moore? For that matter, what was wrong with our dogs? Lassie made them all look like dumbbells (although they didn't seem to care). But we cared. We didn't measure up to the heroines we saw every week on television, and it took years for us to understand that television is fiction—and there were few Ward Cleavers in the world, either. With our minds, we know now that June and Mary were fantasy women. But their image still lingers in our hearts. Oh, how we would like to be as patient and charming and *perfect* as they were! And when we fall short (as we all do), our self-esteem suffers.

The unsettled decade that followed the fifties took a new approach to self-esteem. The sixties made us stop and look at ourselves from a different angle. What did we believe in, and what were we willing to do to back up our beliefs? What made us valuable as women— career, family, or something else? These years never gave us the answers we were looking for, but at least they got us thinking.

Then came the feminist movement, which told us it was time to take charge of our own lives, do what we wanted to do, when we wanted to do it. On the surface, it sounded like a good idea, and no one was unhappy when women's wages began to rise and some of those who had deserved promotions for years finally received them. But those things came at a cost. Suddenly a woman happy in her traditional role of wife and mother was told she was selling herself short. Why wasn't she out there producing like a man? After years of being told it was her job to raise the next generation and find self-esteem in doing so, suddenly she was a failure—a disappointment to all other women if that was all she did. No, now she was supposed to achieve more in the career world. And yet at the same time, she was still responsible for the needs of her family. Fathers may have done more to "help," but the main responsibility for the family's day-to-day well-being still rested squarely on the woman's shoulders. Somehow, she had to do it all.

The truth is, however, no one can do it all, at least not without sacrificing something. If a woman stole time from her family to succeed in business, her self-esteem suffered because she was neglecting what had been her prime work for generations. If she sacrificed her career for the sake of her family, she felt guilt that she was not making good use of her talents and helping her husband provide for the family. She couldn't win either way.

Today women can look for self-esteem in

hundreds of different places. And many women do. New Age ideas are particularly appealing to women, because these "new" thoughts offer comfort and affirmation; they stroke a woman's frail and ailing self-image. But why go to Tibet or learn a shaman's song when what we are looking for is right there in the Bible, in plain English?

In Mary Hollingworth's book *Hugs for Women*, she struggles to define a Christ-centered self-esteem. She uses the term "soul-esteem."

> For several years I've been searching for the right term to replace self-esteem in our vocabulary. I want a word that says, "I can do all things through Christ who gives me the strength." I want a word that says, "God knows that we are made of dust," but "our bodies are the temples of the living God." I want a word that shows that even though we are flawed and weak as human beings, we are strong and capable because the Holy Spirit lives and works through us. I believe that term is soul-esteem.[1]

My own definition of self-esteem is very simple. As a woman, I ask myself, "Am I a person of value?" If my answer is yes, I have self-esteem. If my answer is no—if I truly believe I have little value in this world—my life will be a constant struggle. If I'm not sure about my value, then I will ride the roller coaster of thinking I am fine one day and not so fine the next. If we look at our worth from a human perspective, then we will always see something "flawed and weak." We may feel good about ourselves one day, and terrible the next. But God's perspective is eternal—and by His power, we *can* "do all things."

This doesn't mean, however, that we can literally do everything: hold down a successful career, raise marvelous children, be a great lover, and meet our neighbors' needs, all with serene little smiles on our faces. No, we will always be "made of dust," and our physical frame—not to mention our emotional one—simply can't "do it all." But when our self-esteem is secure through Christ, we will find we have greater wisdom to discern which things God's Spirit is calling us to do—and which things are actually unnecessary. We will be better able to leave our failures (and we all have them) in God's hands, knowing that it is His strength at work in our lives, not our own. He can work all things to His glory, despite our personal weakness.

But a lack of self-esteem can inspire us to be overachievers; it can also lead to many inappropriate or even dangerous behaviors. Anorexia, bulimia, shoplifting, risk taking, drug or alcohol abuse, sexual promiscuity—all these behaviors and many others have their base in a low sense of self-esteem. As an example, take the compulsive spender. What exactly is her problem? Is it money—or is that just the way a lack of self-esteem shows up in her?

Karen O'Connor understands the dangers of low self-esteem:

> Believing that somehow we aren't enough—not pretty enough, thin enough, sexy enough, patient enough. Enough, whatever that is, we aren't it. Deep in our guts we honestly believe that we're defective in some way that can never be fixed. . . . Bankruptcy doesn't work because being in debt is not really a money issue. It is an issue of self-esteem and our feelings of not being

enough, doing enough, or having enough. Women in debt try to fill the emptiness inside by spending money on themselves or others.[2]

A woman who has a right sense of self-esteem is both confident and humble. You know women like this. What a blessing they are! They are full of the strength of the Lord, because they are freed from fears and doubts about their own worth.

I can't help but think of Corrie ten Boom as an example of this kind of person. This Dutch woman put herself in danger to protect dozens of Jews during World War II by hiding them in her house and helping them escape to the countryside. When their good works were discovered, her whole family was sent to a concentration camp. Corrie was the only member of her family to survive the experience.

In her speaking and writing after the war, Corrie freely admitted she was far from perfect. In fact, she went to great lengths to point out her personal faults and failures. Yet when others needed her help, she did not wring her hands and say, "There's nothing I can do!" She had the confidence to step out in faith and accomplish something of value.[3] After the war, she dedicated herself to spreading God's message all over the world, traveling and speaking until she became physically incapable of carrying on any longer. Corrie knew what God wanted her to do with her life and willingly obeyed His directions because, although she knew she was unable, God was able to touch others through her life.

Let me say at the outset, though, that self-esteem is not the same as self-preservation. Self-preservation is an inborn defense we (and even animals) have, to prevent us from putting ourselves in unnecessary danger. It comes with the whole package of life, and is not a character trait or something we have to seek out. Certainly it interacts with self-esteem—only someone with low self-esteem puts themselves in unnecessary danger—but it is only one small part of self-esteem. God is not looking for martyrs. He expects us to protect ourselves whenever possible, to act wisely and with caution. Some people do put themselves at risk for the sake of God, but they are special cases. On the whole, we are not to seek self-esteem through endangering ourselves.

Neither is self-esteem the same as self-love. Self-love turns inward, away from others.

True self-esteem, however, turns outward to others. In Mark 12:31, Jesus says, "Love your neighbor as yourself." Jesus knew how much we care for ourselves, and He was telling us we must feel just as much love for those around us as we do for ourselves. A woman who has found a biblical perspective on self-esteem is secure enough to serve others, to care for them as much as she cares for herself. She is not selfish, focused on her own self and her own life.

Hannah Whitall Smith, author of *The Christian's Secret of a Happy Life*, warns us that when we put our own wants and needs ahead of every other consideration,

> There is never any "profit" in it, but always a grievous loss, and it can never turn out to be anything but "vanity and vexation of spirit." Have we not all discovered something of this in our own experience? You have set your heart, perhaps, on procuring something for the benefit or pleasure of your own great big ME; but when you have secured it, this ungrateful ME has refused to be satisfied, and has

turned away from what it has cost you so much to procure, in weariness and disgust. Never, under any circumstances, has it really in the end paid you to try and exalt your great exacting ME, for always, sooner or later, it has all proved to be "nothing but vanity and vexation of spirit."[4]

The New International Version calls "vanity and vexation of spirit" a "meaningless chasing after the wind" (Eccles. 1:14). Self-love is like chasing the wind; it's a meaningless waste of time. It gets us absolutely nowhere. It certainly doesn't get us real self-esteem.

Does that mean I am to hate myself? Didn't Jesus say, "If anyone comes to me and does not hate. . .even his own life—he cannot be my disciple" (Luke 14:26)? Well, we need to understand the context of Jesus' words, so we can comprehend what He was really saying. When Jesus made that statement, He was using a form of comparison that was very common in His day. What He is saying is that the love we have for God is to be so great that any other love seems like hatred in comparison. But how could it possibly be right for me to hate myself if God considered me valuable enough to give His Son so I can spend eternity with Him? If God loves me that much, if I am that precious to Him, how can I possibly hate myself?

John R. W. Stott, in an article in *Christianity Today,* answered the question, "Am I supposed to love myself or hate myself?" He says "a satisfactory answer cannot be given *without reference to the Cross,*" (italics mine). He adds, "The cross of Christ supplies the answer, for it calls us both to self-denial and to self-affirmation" (which he points out is not the same as self-love). Says Stott, "It is only when we look at the cross that we see the true worth of human beings."[5]

If you don't remember any other sentence in this book, I hope you will remember that last one. It is the cross that reveals my true value—and yours. You will find that nearly every chapter in this book mentions the cross of Jesus and His sacrifice for us, because the cross turns all that is negative in my life into something positive. The cross shows me how bad my sins are and does away with them. The cross—in an astounding, mind-boggling way—shows my true worth as God sees it. Only when we understand the price God was willing to pay to forgive us can we feel right about ourselves and experience healthy, biblical self-acceptance.

Dr. W. David Hager, in his book *As Jesus Cared for Women,* summarizes some of the things we've talked about in this chapter, things that hurt our self-esteem as women:

> The culture of the '90s is full of
> convoluted and conflicting messages.
> Extreme feminism, New Age spirit-
> ualism, and societal immorality
> scream from all directions, leading
> to an identity conflict and recurrent
> questions. "Should I follow career or
> personhood or marriage?" "Should I
> be strong or coy?" "Should I work
> outside the home?" "Can I be satis-
> fied in life as a single person?"
> Because their pace of life is so hec-
> tic, many women never pause long
> enough to make careful decisions
> about these matters. Only a loving
> heavenly Father can lead them
> through the frantic maze and into
> a place of peace and grace. It is
> difficult to hear His voice, however,

when they are burdened by excessive demands of work, family, and friends. It takes time to listen to God, but these times of meditation are important because this is when God can impress upon the listener that her true worth and value is found in the intimacy of her relationship with Him.[6]

My prayer is that as you read this book, you will use this as a time of meditation—a time when you can become more intimate with God. When you do, I know you will hear His quiet voice whispering to your heart, "I love you, daughter. You are precious to Me."

*For God so loved the world
that he gave his one and only Son,
that whoever believes in him
shall not perish but have eternal life.*
JOHN 3:16

We get so caught up in looking at life from our limited, human perspective, that we become blind to what is *real*. The Bible tells us that God values us so much that He gave His only Son so that we can live forever. That's how valuable we are, now and forever.

So compared to that eternal and awesome truth, our own estimations of value don't amount to much. I may not have the face or figure that would ever launch a thousand ships—but who cares? God loves me. I may not be gifted or talented—but what difference does that make? God thought I was worth the price of His only Son. My relationships may all seem like failures right now, and my house is shabby and rundown, and I hate my clothes—but how can that possibly compare to the knowledge that God loves me so much He wants me to live with Him forever?

Over and over the New Testament tells us the same message: Jesus loves us so much He gave His life for us.

Going Further. . .

1. When you see television shows from the fifties, do women like June Cleaver and Mary Tyler Moore trigger an emotional response in you? If so, what is it (guilt, resentment, envy, anger, shame, longing)? Try holding this reaction up to God. Let Him into your heart to heal whatever hurt caused this response.

2. How has the feminist movement helped women? How has it hurt us?

3. In your own words, looking at your own life, what is the difference between self-esteem and self-love?

4. What was something that you did recently that you can see now was motivated by self-love? Did you achieve the goal you hoped for? Or did you turn out to be "chasing the wind"?

5. Whenever you see a cross during the next few days (on church steeples, around people's necks, in stained glass windows) remind yourself that the cross (the cross of Jesus Christ, that is) reveals to you your true worth. Say a simple prayer in your heart thanking Jesus for His love.

Lord, sometimes I can't help but feel confused about the difference between self-esteem and self-love. I get so many different messages, all telling me conflicting things. My own heart is full of all sorts of mixed-up feelings, from resentment to guilt to pride. I know I spend a lot of time "chasing the wind," trying to satisfy my self-love.

Loving God, help me always remember that my only true worth is found in You. Thank You for the gift of Your Son; thank You for loving me so much that You thought I was worth Christ's life. Help me never to forget the cross.

AMEN

CHAPTER 2

*J*UST BE YOURSELF!

An Introvert, an Extrovert, or What?

Have *I* ever struggled with issues of self-esteem, you ask? Absolutely! Especially in the area of being an introvert or an extrovert. While I was growing up, the women I admired were the extroverts. I had the impression that if you were an introvert, you would never be as important or valuable as the woman who was always selected as the leader—the one with the great personality and good public speaking ability, the one who never knew a stranger. In my mind, the extrovert had more value than the introvert.

I didn't realize that we arrive in this world with certain God-given abilities and talents—and each ability or talent is needed. Whether we are extroverted or introverted matters very little. What matters is what we do with whatever gifts God gave us.

As an adult, I have taken several personality profile tests. I know now that I am a combination of both introvert and extrovert, with the needle on the scale leaning clearly toward the introvert. Is that bad? Does that mean I am of less value than if I were an extrovert? No! You see, our society has attached negative ideas to the word "introvert." But those negative connotations have no basis in reality. Clearly we need to understand what each word means.

In simple terms, an extrovert is one who draws her energy from being with people. She may be dog-tired at the end of the day, hardly able to put one foot in front of the other—but she has a party to attend that night, so she reluctantly takes a shower, dresses, and drives to the party. Four hours later, the extrovert, who was so tired she could hardly drag herself there, is one of the last to leave. She is vibrant and full of energy, wide-awake and charming to the end. Why? Because she drew energy from being with people. Social activity recharges her batteries.

How about the introvert? She too received an invitation to the same party. She gets there, enjoys talking intimately with one or two close friends, and thirty minutes later she is wishing she could go home. The longer the evening goes, the more tired she is. Instead of being recharged by the party, it drains her energy. But the next night she has an evening at home to herself, and she works on plans to redecorate her apartment. The hours slip by until she looks up at the clock and finds it is midnight. Yet she is more revitalized than when she began. She draws her energy from entirely different sources than the extrovert.

But we can never say that the extrovert's life is more meaningful than the introvert's; they're just different. If it weren't for extroverts, life would certainly be boring. We'd have fewer parties and clubs and family reunions. We'd laugh a lot less and be a lot lonelier. We might never learn to work together or bear each other's burdens. After all, extroverts are good at social interaction; they help us all get along better. On the other hand, if it weren't for introverts, much less scientific research might be done. Intricate art might go unfinished, because the extrovert did not have the patience to complete it. Certain complex computer programs might never be written, because the picky, long-term work of life depends on introverts. Most important, being an introvert or extrovert may influence your popularity, but it has nothing to do with your value in God's sight.

A twenty-seven-year-old woman who was a single missionary in Indonesia wrote of the struggle she had with this issue. The first year she worked overseas she lived with a young woman named Judy, whom she described as an extrovert, the exact opposite of herself. Judy was a "people-person," whereas she was a quiet person who liked things neat, liked to putter in the kitchen, and enjoyed an evening curled up with a good book.

> *I envied Judy because she is outgoing and I'm not. She can make friends easily; I can't. Neither of us could accept the other, and our tensions affected others. Now I have my own apartment. But if I were to be in a situation where self-acceptance would become a problem, I would fall. The thing that people kept telling me is, "Be yourself. Don't try to be like someone else." But no one would tell me how to be myself. My question is, how can a person be herself?*

Yes, it's easy to say, "Just be yourself." But

in order to do that, we must accept ourselves as we are—the way God made us—believing that if God had wanted us to be a different kind of person, He would have created us that way. Although I still feel insecure and inadequate in certain situations, let me share an experience that went a long way toward helping me work through this issue.

"Lisa needs a place to live for a few months. What do you think about inviting her to live with us?" My husband, never one to waste time when making decisions, waited for my answer. Thoughts raced through my mind. Lisa was beautiful! So beautiful, in fact, that she had been Miss California—twice!

I'm not sure my husband knew he had touched on an old insecurity of mine. I had always felt uncomfortable as a young person when I was around beautiful, graceful, outgoing women. My strength was always making good grades, not entering beauty contests (though I hasten to add that the Miss America Pageant looks for many qualities besides beauty). No doubt these lovely women made me uncomfortable because I judged my worth by comparing myself to them. I never felt I could measure up to their beauty and poise—and as a result, my self-esteem suffered. Now I would be living in the same house with the very kind of woman whose loveliness evoked my childhood insecurities. Well, it was time for me to grow up!

Lisa did live with us. In those six months I learned that she was not only beautiful, but she also had the inward beauty of a humble, quiet spirit. I'm not sure even yet that she, or even my husband, knows she helped me learn to accept myself for who I am.

We can learn skills to make ourselves more effective in life, such as how to make friends or how to value quiet time, or to dress in colors that bring out the best in us. Each of us can be strengthened in our areas of weakness; it is not only futile but wrong to try to change ourselves into what we are not. Let God use the raw materials He created in you to accomplish His purpose for your life.

Luci Swindoll, in her book *You Bring the Confetti*, calls us to be "genuine in Christ."

> We are the most appealing to
> others and the happiest within,
> when we are completely ourselves.
> But it is a constant struggle

because, as Scripture teaches, the world is always trying to press us into its mold. The mold of the world is the mold of the synthetic, the mold of the artificial, the mold of the celluloid—the "Plastic Person."

The world cries, "You've got to be young and you've got to be tan. You've got to be thin and you've got to be rich. You've got to be great." But Scripture says, "You don't have to be any of those things. You simply have to be yourself—at any age—as God made you, available to Him so that He can work in and through you to bring about His kingdom and His glory." Now relax. Trust Him and be yourself![1]

At the beginning of this chapter, I said that what matters is not whether we are extroverts or introverts, but what we do with whatever gifts God has given us. Extroverted or introverted, we need to put our personalities in God's hands—and He will use us to His glory.

We also need to remember that even the extrovert has her weaknesses. Perhaps she may even need a little of the introvert's quiet strength. Listen to this quote from Ruthe White's book, *A Spiritual Diary for Saints and Not-So-Saintly*:

I'm tired of being strong! Weary of being a leaning post. If people really knew how weak I was, they would never look to me for support.

But I'm afraid to tell them!

Afraid to let them know I hurt, too. I don't want anyone to know I struggle with some of the same problems everyone else does. It makes me look so good, so spiritual, to pretend.

Have I made myself appear to others as a great pillar of strength, a spiritual authority standing with outstretched arms, inviting people to look up to me?

I dare not tell them what I really am! . . . If they only knew how fragile I was, how easily broken, they would never believe in me again.

Perhaps, perhaps not!

Maybe confession is what is needed. To allow myself to be exposed. Broken! Then there would be no reason for others to come to me or hold me in esteem.

Yes, that is it. Brokenness is what is needed —to lose the pieces of my own identity! Let self be lost so a new person can emerge.

One that is honest, glued together with love, unafraid to be exposed and obviously human.[2]

Sometimes we all need to risk admitting our own insecurities and weaknesses. That's the only way we'll be able to help each other, sharing our individual strengths with one another.

God accepts us just as we are. He does not ask us to measure up to anyone else's standards. All He asks is that we put all He has given us, whatever that is, back in His hands.

In fact, God has arranged the parts
in the body, every one of them,
just as he wanted them to be.
If they were all one part,
where would the body be?
As it is, there are many parts,
but one body.
1 CORINTHIANS 12:18–20

Obviously, the apostle Paul understood
the way people think. Even back in the
early church, he knew that people
would be comparing themselves to each
other, wondering why they couldn't
have the same gifts and abilities that
someone else had. He understood that
people's self-esteem would all too often
be wounded as they looked around the
church at the many talented and out-
standing people.

To help heal these wounds to self-
esteem, Paul used a human body as his
illustration. He wanted us to understand the way God sees us. When we

look at another person and think, *She's so much more outgoing than I am, so she must be worth more to God,* that makes as much sense as it would if your foot got all upset because it couldn't be your hand. Or if we look at a gifted leader and think, *Compared to her, I'm nothing, so I might just as well give up*, that's as silly as if your ear started crying because it couldn't be an eye, insisting that it might as well just walk away and leave your body altogether. Imagine a body that was all one big eye. What a useless monstrosity that would be!

The point Paul is making is this: We all need each other. Your hand is just as dependent on your eye as your eye is on your hand—and your head needs your feet as much as your feet need your head. We are all part of the body that is the Church.

We each need to offer up our special strengths for the good of Christ's Body. And at the same time, we need to acknowledge our weaknesses, both to ourselves and to others, so that we can draw from the special strengths of others. Christ doesn't want there to be any division in His Body.

This is how Paul puts it:

If one part suffers,
every part suffers with it;
if one part is honored,
every part rejoices with it.
Now you are the body of Christ,
and each one of you is a part of it.
(1 CORINTHIANS 12:26–27)

GOING FURTHER. . .

1. What qualities do you admire most about an extrovert? What do you admire most about the introvert?

2. Are these qualities that you possess? Or are they talents that you *wish* you had?

3. Do you think of yourself as an introvert or an extrovert? Why?

4. What strengths do you see in your personality? How could these gifts be put to use for God's Kingdom?

5. Do you find it difficult to admit your weaknesses to others? Why?

6. Why is it important to be honest with each other about our shortcomings and weaknesses?

Dear Jesus, thank You for giving me the gift of myself. Remind me that You will never ask me to be anyone but who I am. Help me not to measure myself against the gifts and abilities of others.

Thank You, Lord, that I can be part of Your Body. I give to You my whole self, for You to use. Sometimes it seems to me like I don't have much to offer—but I know when I think like that, I'm forgetting that You made me just the way You wanted me to be. I put myself in Your hands. Please use me for the good of Your entire living Body.

AMEN

CHAPTER 3

A MISTAKE OR A MASTERPIECE?

A Woman's Basis for Self-Esteem

"All my life I've struggled with being too tall," my friend confided to me. From the day she started school, she was a foot taller than anyone else in her class. At the end of the school day she would run home crying, trying to escape the taunts of the other children. People stared at her, she told me, as if she were some kind of freak. When she was thirteen, her parents put her in the hospital for hormone treatments to stop her growth, but they were unsuccessful. To make matters worse, people often compared her to her younger sister, who was of average height and considered prettier than she. My friend grew up feeling she was a big mistake.

Struggling with a lack of self-esteem, she began to compensate for her tallness in various ways. She got good grades, became proficient in four languages, achieved in athletics, and eventually won a law degree and began a successful career. But underlying all her achievement was the gnawing feeling that God had made a mistake when He made her. This feeling affected everything she did. More importantly, it affected her attitude toward God, whom she could not see as a loving, perfect Father. To her, God was not perfect—not when He had made such mistakes when He made her.

Are you struggling with the same feelings? For you, being tall may not be a problem. Perhaps instead you have an emotional problem or disability. Or maybe your outlook on life has been warped by parents who constantly told you that you were no good, that you would never amount to anything in life—and you still believe them. Possibly you've committed some sin that you feel has disqualified you for a life of value and purpose, and you have never forgiven yourself. Perhaps you are a victim of rape or incest or some other set of horrible circumstances that you had no control over but still feel guilt about. Whatever happened to you in the past, the end result is that you don't think very highly of yourself. You have given up trying to be all that you could be. *What's the use?* you think. Perhaps you have also given up on God, believing that somewhere in your life He made a horrible mistake.

As my friend and I talked about the physical problem that had so strongly influenced her sense of worth, I turned to her and asked, "Have you ever considered the possibility that God wanted you to be tall, that it's not a mistake or merely a genetic quirk that you are tall?"

She didn't answer right away, so I went on. "I think that God allowed you to be tall because He wanted a tall frame for the work of art that He is making of your life—the masterpiece, no less, that He wants to create in you. You know that every artist likes to choose the frame that best displays his work. It is not a mistake that you are tall. If God had wanted you to be 5'5" tall, He would have made you that way. You are not a mistake. You are the canvas on which He wants to display beauty, and your body is the frame for the Artist's work."

Can you apply what I said to my friend to your own life? It may be that the very thing you hate most about yourself is actually the canvas God needed for the beautiful work of art He plans to create out of your life. I know that accepting a concept like this means you have to look at yourself in an entirely new way—and that won't be easy, particularly if you've been hating something about yourself for years, maybe even for your entire life. But try to shift your perspective until you can look at yourself from God's viewpoint. You might be surprised by what you see.

I'm not saying here, however, that every bad thing that has happened to you has been God's will for your life. Some things have come about through the actions of others or the actions of nature, so blaming God for every bad thing in your life is unfair. He has given us free will and great latitude in our actions, and there are people in the world who take advantage of their free will to hurt the lives of others. I cannot fully explain the effect of sin and evil in this world—and in your life and mine—apart from the fact that Satan has been given limited domain in this world for a period of time. Men and women, starting with Adam and Eve, have yielded to his temptations, with the result that until Christ returns and destroys Satan, we will struggle with both the power and the effects of sin in this world.

But the redemptive fact is that God has said, "My grace is sufficient for you, for my power is made perfect in weakness" (2 Corinthians 12:9). He can take the broken pieces of any life and create out of them a work of art that will bring glory to Him and blessing to others. He can take even the wounds dealt to you by both circumstances and others, and use them for His glory. So long as you put yourself in God's hands, nothing can keep Him from turning your life into the beautiful creation He always intended it to be.

No matter what you are today—or what you were in the past—you are not a mistake. You are a potential work of art in which God wants to reveal His power, glory, love, and creativity. God can take your suffering and turn it into a blessing for yourself and others. Don't hold a grudge against God. Let Him work with you as you are and turn your life into the masterpiece He has planned for it.

The first step in seeing yourself as God sees you—as a person of worth and value—is to take a look at the canvas on which He wants to create this masterpiece, so you can understand who you are. When you understand just who you truly are, you'll have a clearer idea of what God's perspective on your life really is. That's what we're going to do in the next chapter.

P.S. As I have been writing this, my tall friend has been at the shopping center buying her first pair of high heels!

*There was given to me a thorn in
my flesh, a messenger of Satan,
to torment me.
Three times I pleaded with the Lord
to take it away from me.
But he said to me,
"My grace is sufficient for you,
for my power is made perfect
in weakness."
Therefore I will boast
all the more gladly about my weaknesses,
so that Christ's power may rest on me. . . .
For when I am weak, then I am strong.*
2 CORINTHIANS 12:7–10

Just think—even Paul the apostle had
something about himself that hurt
him, something that he wished God
would just take away. We don't know
what that thing was, although Bible
experts have had all sorts of theories.
It might have been an illness or some
sort of physical disability; it may even
have been a personality problem; but

whatever it was, Paul felt it made him less than perfect. And he asked God to take this "thorn of the flesh" away from him.

Do you have "thorns" that torment you, too? Almost everyone does, of one sort or another. Each person's particular flaw or weakness is different—but whatever it is, it acts as a messenger from Satan. It whispers to us, "You're not good enough. A person with *this* problem will never accomplish much of anything. You just don't measure up."

Satan certainly can use that thorn to torment us. But guess what? God can use it, too—but in an entirely different way. He will use that ugly, painful thorn for His glory.

That's why when Paul prayed that his personal "thorn in the flesh" be taken away, God told him "No" three times, until Paul finally got the message. At last, Paul understood that the very thing that hurt him so much, the thing that Satan had been using to speak his lies, that same awful thing was the very opportunity that Christ needed to show His power and grace in Paul's life.

If we could do everything perfectly, eventually we'd get pretty arrogant. If we thought nothing about us could be improved, we wouldn't think we needed God at all; we'd assume we could do everything in our own strength, without any help from Him. That's why Paul says that when he is weak he is strong. The very thing that reminds us of our own imperfection can also be the thing that turns us to God. And whenever we acknowledge our own weakness, God has the chance to pour out His strength in our lives.

The secret is to refuse to listen to Satan's lies. Instead, turn to God immediately whenever your "thorn" jabs you. Despite your weakness—no, *because* of your weakness—Christ's power will rest on you.

1. Have you ever felt that God made a mistake in the way He made you? Have you felt He made a mistake when He allowed some circumstance to happen in your life? Are you still angry at God about this?

2. Can you think of ways that God has already or may yet turn that "mistake" into a blessing? Look at your life prayerfully and write them down. Whenever you get discouraged with yourself, read the list over to remind yourself that God is working in your life.

3. Is there something in your life that you still can't see as a potential blessing? Write it down—and then pray every day that God will show you a way that He can use this "mistake" to His glory and your blessing. He *will* answer your prayer—and when He does, make sure you write down whatever new

insight He has shown you. (Satan will be all too ready to make your "blessing" look like a "mistake" again, so it's good to have a written record.)

4. Write Psalm 139:14 on a note card and tape it on your bathroom or vanity mirror.

Dear God, You know the thing I like least about myself. You know how long I have struggled with feelings of insecurity and self-doubt because of this thing. I'm not sure I can bring myself yet to thank You for making me this way, not when I hate this thing so much.

But Father, I know You don't make mistakes. And I know You were there when I was being created inside my mother's womb, and You've been there every day since then. And I know You love me.

So, dear God, I put myself in Your hand—all of me, even this thing about myself that I don't like very much. Please use me to Your glory. Use even this thing that I hate. Maybe someday I'll be able to see Your plan. And in the meantime, I'll trust You.

Go ahead, God—create a work of art in my life.

AMEN

CHAPTER 4

WHO, WHERE, WHY?

*Women and Life's
Basic Questions*

And now for the four great questions of life:

Who am I?
Where did I come from?
Why am I here?
Where am I going?

Down through the centuries, people have sought the answers to these four questions. Philosophers have pondered and debated them. Historians have searched the past for clues. Astrologers have looked for signs in the skies to guide them. Ordinary and extraordinary people have shouted these questions into the cold night sky and whispered them into their pillows.

Sometimes we feel we have found the

answer to one or two of these questions, but they soon prove to be only partial answers, unsatisfactory when circumstances change. We read and study philosophy or theology, hoping to find the answers there—and we come away confused and baffled. It's like beating our heads against the wall; if these questions are universal, as they seem to be, there must be an answer to them somewhere—but where? Most of us finally give up, deciding that these answers are not available to us in this lifetime.

I am no theologian or philosopher, but I do believe the answers to these four questions are found in the Bible, which was written by the One who created both us and the world we live in. Only He knows the answers, and He has told us all we need to know.

To accept ourselves as people of value, we need to know what God says about these four gigantic questions. If we don't know who we are, where we came from, why we are here, and where we are going, how can we ever accept ourselves or even begin to live the lives God wants us to live?

Let's see what the Bible says about these questions, one by one.

Who Am I?

1. YOU ARE A COMPLETELY UNIQUE INDIVIDUAL. Among all the other 3.5 billion women in the world, there is no one exactly like you. No one else sees with your eyes, hears with your ears, thinks your thoughts, or feels what you feel. You are one of a kind. Regardless of how you were conceived—whether you were an "accident" or the gift of life cherished and longed for by the two people who gave you life—you were created by God's will. It was God who deigned to give you life when 500,000 sperm competed with one another to fertilize the ovum and made you who you are. Just think of this: If another sperm had won the race, you would not be you! You would be a sister to yourself, similar in some ways to who you are now, but also uniquely different. Have no doubt about it, you were meant to be born, and you were meant to be exactly who you are. Your identity is the result of neither coincidence nor accident. You are who you are because of God's loving design. He wanted you to be *you*, and no one else.

2. YOU WERE CREATED IN THE IMAGE OF GOD. How do you respond to that statement? Do you

believe it with your head—but not with your heart? All of your sins and flaws and failures whisper to you, "*You're* not much like God." If you listen, you'll be overwhelmed with discouragement and self-hatred. Your heart will feel too dark to ever contain the brilliance of God's image.

But at some point, wrote C. S. Lewis, you have to tell your emotions where to get off. You have to disregard your feelings of inadequacy and inferiority, and accept what God says about you. Did you ever stop to think about the power of the verse that says you were created in the image of God? Because you are created in His image, you have the power to think, to reason, to converse, and to live forever. Unlike lower forms of life, you can express yourself in ways that come only through the touch of the divine on your life.

At creation, God made Adam from the dust of the ground. Then He took a rib from Adam to make Eve. Notice that Adam wasn't the only one made in God's image. So was Eve. Genesis 1:27 tells us, "So God created man in his own image. . .male and female he created them." It follows, then, that. . .

3. YOU ARE A WOMAN DESCENDED FROM EVE, WHO WAS CREATED FROM ADAM'S RIB BY THE HAND OF GOD—AND THEREFORE DOUBLY REFINED AT CREATION.

The story goes that after God made Adam, He looked him over and said, "I can do better than that!" and He made a woman! Be that as it may, after God made Adam from the dust of the ground, He took one of Adam's ribs and, according to the literal rendering of the Hebrew text, "built He a woman."

This double refinement resulted in remarkable differences between men and women. Shortly after we were married, my husband Harold accepted the fact that as a woman I have an intuitive feel for things that he just doesn't have. He's better on geographic directions—how to get from one place to another in a strange city—but when it comes to people, I have a feel for situations and I sense vibes that go right over his head. He doesn't consider this a threat to his manhood; instead he recognizes that God has given us different talents and abilities.

In the 1980s, while feminists were trying to wipe out the lines of demarcation between males and females, scientists discovered that there are rather radical differences in the brain development of prenatal males and females. The left side of the brain of a little girl develops more quickly than that of her brother. This results in an ability to better express herself verbally than her male counterparts. "We use the left brain," says Dr. Joyce Brothers, "when we balance our checkbook, read a newspaper, sing a song, play bridge, write a letter."[1]

This produces intuitive reasoning and sensitivity, something men don't have in the same way. Unborn female babies recognize their mothers' voices sooner than do male babies, and after they are born, they can identify faces sooner than their brothers can. On the other hand, the dominant right side of the male brain grasps the larger picture, which may account for the fact that men usually excel at tasks requiring logical sequences—computers, engineering, architecture, and so forth. (Obviously, I'm speaking in generalities here. I'm not saying that no women are good at computers or engineering, nor is *every* man good at these things. I'm merely speaking of general, across-the-board tendencies.)

The way that men and women process information is different, as well. My husband contends that women process information like video cameras—recording every detail—while men are more like single-lens reflex cameras, shooting one scene at a time and missing a lot of details. Between the two of us, my husband and I, each working in our own way, we develop a pretty complete picture of any situation.

But being different has nothing to do with being superior or inferior. Sexual differences are all part of God's design and purpose for our lives, something many cultures (and many men) have never grasped. The ancient rabbis, who thanked God that they were neither Gentiles nor women, just didn't get it. When it comes to being a person of value, no one sex has the advantage. Both patriarchy and matriarchy fail to show a complete picture of God's will.

4. You are a sinner who fell short of God's expectations.

This is not gender specific; it is true of us all. The Bible says simply, "We all, like sheep, have gone astray, each of us has turned to his own way; and the Lord has laid on him the iniquity of us all" (Isaiah 53:6). Because I am a woman, I am no more a saint than a male, nor less a sinner. "All have sinned," is Paul's dictum (Romans 3:23). Sin is an equal-opportunity failing.

5. Because of God's love in Christ Jesus, if you have put your trust in Him, you are a new person, God's child. This means:

You are adopted into God's family; you are the daughter of the King. This is not poetic license. It's a fact. Every mother loves her child, but an infant who is adopted is doubly loved because of a decision—a conscious act of the will—to be a mother to that particular child. This is what God says He has done for us.

"Why is God punishing my baby for what I did?" a young mother asked my husband Harold, with scalding tears pouring down her cheeks. Her baby was lying in a crib, a tiny little girl not expected to live beyond the age of two because she had been born with five holes in her heart.

Was God punishing this child for the series of sexual encounters her mother had before she was married, before she heard the Good News and became a believer? No, not if you believe what the Bible says about forgiveness. God said, "I, yes, I alone am he who blots away your sins for my own sake and will never think of them again" (Isaiah 43:25, TLB). When God forgives, He wipes the slate clean, as though you had never sinned. He certainly does not punish your children for sins you committed—sins He forgave you for as soon as you asked His forgiveness.

(Incidentally, my husband prayed that God would heal the holes in the tiny heart of that infant, so her mother would know that when God forgives, He forgets our sins. The last time we had contact with them, the little baby had become a young adult who was enjoying excellent health.)

Where Did I Come From?

As we discussed in the last chapter, the phrases of Psalm 139:13–16 tell us that each of us is individually formed and therefore unique: "You created my inmost being; you knit me together in my mother's womb. . . . My frame was not hidden from you when I was made in the secret place. When I was woven together. . .your eyes saw my unformed body. All the days ordained for me were written in your book before one of them came to be."

How do these truths relate to my sense of self-esteem? Let's put these facts together and see what they imply. First of all, God created me in His image. Being created in God's image means that I'm patterned after the original model. Amazing! God didn't have to do that; He wanted to. Even though through His fore-knowledge He knew that I—along with every human being who ever lived since Adam and Eve—would rebel against Him, He still made me. I have value to God.

God literally knit or wove me together in my mother's womb. Whether or not I like my personal appearance, the fact that God put me together means that He has a purpose for me, just as I am. No one in all the world—no one who has lived or ever will live—is exactly the same as me. I may wish that He had made me more like someone else. I may feel that if I were more like someone else, I would be of more value. But if God had wanted someone like that person, He would have created me that way. I am the person I am because God wanted someone just like me.

As Rick Warren puts it, I have a God-given SHAPE unlike that of any other person:[2]

> S—spiritual gifts
> H—heart desires
> A—abilities
> P—personality
> E—life experiences

The truth is that He has a purpose for me as I am. I may never in my entire lifetime understand why I am like I am, but God has a purpose for me that will glorify Him—and that makes me a person of value.

In *Hugs for Women*, Mary Hollingsworth speaks of our unique roles in God's kingdom.

> God needs you, too. Whatever gifts and abilities He gave you, He needs you to be at work in His world and His kingdom. No one else can do what He designed you for in the same way you can.
>
> No one else can play your role. No one else knows your lines. You are uniquely created to fit in the special you-shaped space God formed in His world.[3]

But I am not merely an unduplicated snowflake of God's creation, special simply because I am unique. No, I am far more valuable than that, because God loves me. In fact, He loves me so much that at great personal cost He did what was necessary so that I could have fellowship with Him: He sent His only Son, Jesus Christ, to earth to die on the cross to pay the penalty that I deserved to pay for my sins—death.

Am I worth the price God paid for me? I don't think so—but He does. God's desire for fellowship with me is so great that He did the unthinkable: He put His holy, beloved Son through the agony of crucifixion. If you ever doubt that you are valuable, read John 3:16 again and remind yourself of the price He paid for you: "For God so loved the world that he gave his one and only Son, that whoever believes in him shall not perish but have eternal life."

Why Am I Here?

Eve was created to be a helper to Adam. In Genesis 2:18 God said it was not good for the man to be alone. "I will make a helper suitable for him." I once heard Fay Angus say that when God made Adam, then took a good look at him, He said, "Heavenly days, he certainly could use some help!" So He made Eve.

Maybe that's going a little far. But we do know that you and I were made by God's will. "You [God] created all things, and by your will they were created" (Revelation 4:11). We also know that we were created to bring glory to

God, because He says of those who are called by His name, "whom I created for my glory" (Isaiah 43:7).

That's pretty high and mighty for me! Maybe some day I'll comprehend what it really means. I can understand, however, that what I do is important when God says, "Let your light shine before men, that they may see your good deeds and praise your Father in heaven" (Matthew 5:16), or when He says, in Ephesians 2:10, "For we are God's workmanship, created in Christ Jesus to do good works, which God prepared in advance for us to do."

Biblical self-esteem takes the spotlight off me and puts it on Jesus. I am here on earth for Him, not for me. Scripture is clear about this. "He died for all, that those who live should no longer live for themselves but for him who died for them" (2 Corinthians 5:15). My job is to learn what God wants me to do for Him.

This is not necessarily an easy task. Do you struggle with knowing God's will for your life? Perhaps the easiest way to approach the task is by the process of elimination. Through careful Bible study, we can begin to understand what God does *not* want us to be. That still leaves us a lot of possibilities, however. God does not hand us a list of chores to be done and say, "Pick one." It would certainly be simpler if He did, but God is not a big personnel office in the sky. Given our personal talents and abilities, we must decide what we are to do with our lives. Whatever we choose, the point is that we are to serve God with our lives, to put Him and His Kingdom first. A dishwasher can do that just as well as a member of the Board of Directors.

Where Am I Going?

This last question is the scariest to the nonbeliever and the most wonderful to one who trusts in Christ. When life is over, if I have a personal relationship with Jesus, I am going to be with God. Think of the wonder of these phrases: "I [Jesus] will come back and take you to be with me that you also may be where I am" (John 14:2–3); ". . .we will be with him forever" (2 Thessalonians 4:16–17); ". . .at home with the Lord" (2 Corinthians 5:6–8).

Because Christ gave Himself for us, the very least we can do for Him is to offer our lives in gratitude, to be used as He sees fit. The problem comes when we say, "How could God possibly use my life? Oh yes, He uses the missionaries and the talented people. But me? I'm just an ordinary person. I can't do much for God."

Notice that God doesn't ask us to bring just our talents and abilities and all the "good" things in our lives to Him. He asks us to bring everything in our lives—every part of us—and offer ourselves as a living sacrifice for Him to use as He desires (Romans 12:1–2). Some days we may feel proud of what we have to offer God—but other days, maybe most of our days, we'll feel pretty embarrassed about what we have to give Him. But God really doesn't care either way. He just wants us to lay our lives on His altar.

Do you have a quick temper? Give it to God. Are you clumsy? Put your clumsiness in God's hand. Are you overweight? Offer your body to God as a living sacrifice. Let me repeat myself again: God doesn't want just the "good stuff." He wants it all. And when we give it to Him, He will use it all, good and bad, for His kingdom. Our part is to trust that He is doing just that, whether or not we can see the results.

How can we know how we have affected others in our lifetime? One smile may very well change another person's life. Our children may seem perfectly normal and unremarkable to us, but three generations from now a world leader may come from our family tree. Our happy marriage may very well serve as an example to another couple and prevent a divorce that would have had serious repercussions on the children of that couple. Our volunteer work as mentors might make the difference between a young person experimenting with drugs or becoming the doctor who conquers cancer. One drop of water falling on a rock changes that rock forever.

Some day we are going to be with the Lord forever and ever. I'm convinced that only in heaven will we know the unseen ways in which God has used us to bless those around us and accomplish His purposes. Trust Him to use your life—all of it—as a tool of value in His eternal design.

*But when the time had fully come,
God sent his Son. . .
to redeem those under law,
that we might receive the full rights of
sons. Because you are sons,
God sent the Spirit of his Son
into our hearts,
the Spirit who calls out, "Abba, Father."
So you are no longer a slave, but a son;
and since you are a son,
God has made you also an heir.*
GALATIANS 4:4–7

Eugene Peterson paraphrases Galatians
4:7 as follows: "Doesn't that privilege
of intimate conversation with God
make it plain that you are not a slave,
but a child? And if you are a child
you're also an heir, with complete
access to the inheritance."[4]

The word the apostle Paul used in
describing this adoption into the family
of God was a legal term. According to
Roman law, a person who was adopted

could never be prosecuted for former crimes. She received a new name and literally became a new person. So what does that mean if you are God's adopted child? Well, for one thing, it means you are completely forgiven. You have an entire new identity as God's child. All your old sins belong to the old you—and that person no longer exists. You are a new person in Christ Jesus.

Notice what verse 6 says: "God sent the Spirit of his Son into our hearts." If you grasp that fact, your self-esteem will be radically changed forever. When you give your life to Jesus, He Himself will live inside you. He will be a part of your very heart. And His voice within you will call out to God.

The word *Abba* was the Aramaic word for *Daddy,* a familiar, loving word for a kind and intimate father. When Jesus lives within you, you have the right to call God "Daddy" because you are now His beloved child.

1. Write a few phrases next to the SHAPE acrostic that describe your-self and make you who you are:

   > S-spiritual gifts
   > H-heart desires
   > A-abilities
   > P-personality
   > E-life experiences

2. Now, can you prayerfully place each one on these things of God's altar? Is there anything that's diffi-cult for you to let go? Why?

3. If you had to sum up your answer in one sentence, why do you think God put you on this earth?

4. Do you know for certain where you are going when you die? If not, read chapter 6 right now and settle that issue with God. Then write a sentence or two about your assur-ance of eternal life.

5. Whenever you catch yourself feeling discouraged with yourself, whenever you feel as though you just can't "measure up," say to yourself, *Jesus lives in my heart and I am God's child.*

Jesus, thank You that You hold the answer to all the most important questions in my life. You know who I am, You know where I came from, You know why You put me here, and You know where I am going. Please use me however You want. I lay my whole self on Your altar.

Because of You, Lord, I know I am an entirely new person. Thank You for living in my heart. Thank You that I can call God "Daddy."

AMEN

CHAPTER 5

*H*OW TO PREVENT AN IDENTITY CRISIS

Dealing with Life's Changes

"You must have a perfect body to match your perfect personality," say the media.

"Your home and family must be perfect, too," says society.

"You must succeed in your career," says the professional world.

"You're merely the product of chance," says the theory of evolution, "so what difference does it make what you do?"

Voices all around you clamor for attention, eager to sell you on their particular formula for happiness. You can read how-to books on almost any subject. You can go to seminars and learn how to become rich, beautiful, and successful in anything you want to try. Any information you want can be found on the Internet.

Even a serious seeker of personal help soon becomes a victim of overload. Sometimes you just want to cover your ears and yell, "Let me be me—the imperfect but unique me."

Yet when you lie in bed at night with the lights out, are you comfortable in God's sight with who you are—or do you fall short of your own expectations? Very few people are so secure that they never doubt themselves. We are all sinners and feel inadequate at times. Indeed, being human, we all are inadequate in many ways. When these feelings begin to take control of our lives to the point where we feel inadequate most of the time, we are in the throes of what is often called an identity crisis. How vulnerable are you to this type of thinking?

Follow these three simple steps to find out.

Step 1:

Be honest with yourself about what gives you your sense of self-worth. List the things that are good about you, as well as what you view as important parts of who you are. You must be brutally honest here. Write down not what you think the list should include, but what you honestly believe. You might include:

1. Your appearance (not only beauty but what you do with your appearance—grooming, your sense of style, and so on)
2. Your career or mission in life
3. Your role as a single or married person
4. Your role as a mother
5. What God says about your value (Be careful here. It's easy to write down some Scriptures without making a true evaluation of what has become a reality to you.)
6. What others say about you, including your family (Do verbal strokes make you feel worthwhile?)
7. Your intelligence
8. Your physical fitness
9. Your personality (the ability to make friends and relate to other people)
10. Your character (Do you like living with yourself?)
11. Your skills (social, artistic, and so on)

12. Your achievements, past and present

_____

_____

_____

_____

_____

_____

_____

_____

_____

_____

_____

_____

_____

_____

_____

_____

_____

_____

_____

_____

_____

_____

_____

_____

_____

_____

_____

_____

_____

_____

_____

_____

_____

_____

_____

_____

_____

_____

Now, what else gives you a sense of self-worth?
Write it all down.

_____

_____

_____

_____

_____

_____

_____

_____

_____

_____

_____

_____

_____

_____

_____

_____

_____

_____

_____

_____

What you have jotted down on your list will tell you:

1. Who you are
2. What you do

Step 2:

After you have made your list, ask yourself, "Which of these things can or will be taken away from me at some point in my life?" Put a mark by each source of self-esteem that may change. Again, be honest with yourself. Right now, your marriage may be solid, but could that change in the future? (If nothing else, odds are your husband will die before you do. Sooner or later, most women are widows.) Right now, your young children are wonderful and loving, but will they be the same as teens or young adults? Right now, you may like yourself, but will you feel the same when you grow old and grouchy?

Step 3:

Evaluate your vulnerability. What if your kids don't turn out well, or you become handicapped or disfigured, or poor, or you never marry, or you lose your husband, or. . . ? How would you feel about yourself then? (Some of us are very good at this game; we worry a lot.) If most of your sense of self-worth comes from sources that at some point in life can or will be taken from you, you are vulnerable to an identity crisis.

At some point in your life (often at midlife), you will look in the mirror and discover you no longer have the attention-getting appearance you once had. There will be bags under your eyes, and your waist measurement will be getting too close to your chest measurement for comfort. Marabel Morgan in *Total Joy* speaks of this realization—and offers us comfort.

> Every woman knows she must someday grow old and lose the bloom of youth. Yet when it begins to happen, she registers shock. Wrinkles appear overnight. She sees the law of gravity pulling on her underarms and chin and everything below the chin. Who would have ever thought it could happen to her?
>
> Proverbs Chapter 31 describes

God's Total Woman. One of her chief characteristics is "no fear of old age" because she follows His plan for her, day-by-day. He makes life so great there's not much time to fret about the bags and sags, much less time to fear them.

While my girls and I were talking about life one day, I told them, "Your body is actually a shell, a 'house' you wear. The real you which is inside your body will someday leave. So if anything happens to your body, it won't affect the real you. Even if you were in an accident and your arms or legs were cut off, the real you would still be intact inside."

To me, that's very comforting. Knowing that God designed my house takes great pressure off me. I am not going to fight His design. Someday we'll be free of these bodies and their diseases and limitations, but for now we're stuck inside. I'll change what I can and accept what I can't.[1]

Still, if your self-esteem has been based on your appearance, accepting the effects of time on your looks can be a painful lesson.

About the same time that this is happening to your appearance, your last child will leave home, leaving you with far too much free time and a lack of direction. Eventually you will get up some morning and find that your joints feel stiff. Your eyesight will begin to fail, and you will need at least two pair of glasses. Moreover, you may be hit with the realization that you have not yet achieved the goals you set for yourself in your youth. You will never write that book, run that marathon, or open up that business you have been saving for. Time is running out on you, and you have lost a lot of chances along the way.

Or a major change will come in your life —a death, a physical handicap, career disappointment, or a broken relationship—that will stop you in your tracks and force you to reevaluate yourself. Make no mistake, some of these things happen to us all. How will you cope? Can you prepare yourself in advance for life's inevitable changes?

I do not mean to imply that we do not or should not gain a sense of self-esteem from those around us. The love and praise of those dear to us is a precious gift of encouragement that not only gives us "warm fuzzies" but also does much to contribute to our sense of self-worth. But because life often brings drastic changes, each of us needs a solid, unchangeable foundation for feeling worthwhile. We cannot depend totally on others for our self-worth.

Go back to your list of sources of self-esteem. Do you have anything listed there that will never change? How about what God says about your value? Have the facts of Scripture become an ingrained source of your self-esteem—or are they still theory to you?

One of the saddest letters my husband and I ever received was from a sixty-eight-year-old woman who asked, "How good must I be for God to love me?" Abandoned by her mother at birth and not adopted until she was twelve, this woman had deep emotional scars. She suffered from having grown up believing that acceptance —from other people and from God—is based on our looks, our abilities, and our performance.

At the age of fifteen she attended a church and for the first time heard the salvation message. She responded and received Jesus Christ as her personal Savior, but her joy was overwhelmed by feelings of unworthiness as she went home and knelt by her bed that night. Instead of rejoicing in her new faith, she wept and asked God to let her die, because she knew she could never "stay good enough for God to love me." She closed her sad letter with the question, "Does God perform plastic surgery of the heart to erase the trauma of childhood?"

Paul wrote to the Ephesians, "He [God] has made us accepted in the beloved [Christ]" (Ephesians 1:5, KJV). This means that our acceptance by the Father has nothing to do with our goodness or badness; it totally rests upon what Jesus did. Because God accepts you, you can accept yourself. Because God recognizes you as a person of value and worth, you can recognize yourself as one made in His image, important and worthwhile.

The best way you can protect yourself from a personal crisis is to base your sense of self-worth primarily on the one source that does not change: God. God loves you! John 3:16 says He loves you so much that He gave His only Son for you. Has that truth sunk into your innermost being? Do you really believe that Jesus died for you? It's not hard to believe He died for *us*—collectively—but do you feel He died for *you*—personally? Could

He have loved you that much, when He had a whole world of people to deal with? You think you are one unimportant individual, and sometimes it feels as if He doesn't even know you exist. But He does.

It's a hard fact to grasp. I can't understand why He loves me with such an intense love. In my evaluation of myself, I'm not worth that kind of love. I know my faults very well, and I do not deserve His love. But what I feel about myself has nothing to do with the fact that, despite everything, God loves me—and always will. There is no greater source of self-esteem than that!

No matter what you look like, no matter what you do or don't do, nothing changes the fact that God loves you. The society you live in may say you have little value, but God says you are so valuable to Him that He gave His Son to suffer and be crucified so you—you, the individual—could live with Him forever. That is the bedrock upon which you must build your life and from which you can gain a sense of self-esteem that nothing can destroy.

In a previous chapter, I said you are a work of art that God is creating. How much is a piece of art worth? Well, that depends on what someone is willing to pay for it. Obviously, an art collector would pay a lot more for the *Mona Lisa* than for my absent-minded doodles and scribbles. How much was God willing to pay for you? An enormous price—the life of His only Son, given through an agonizing death! He didn't do that for any other part of His creation. He did it only for those of us made in His image. Whether you feel like it or not, you are supremely valuable to Him—a *Mona Lisa*, not a scribble or doodle. An exquisite work of craftsmanship and beauty.

Sometimes something that's been overlooked as a worthless piece of junk turns out to be more valuable than we would ever have dreamed. Recently Richard Rusthton-Clem of Lewisburg, Pennsylvania, bought an old pickle bottle for three dollars at a tag sale. A few months later he offered it for sale on Ebay, the Internet auction site. Much to his surprise, after a week-long auction and more than sixty bids, the eleven-inch amber bottle sold for $44,100! Some mornings do you wake up feeling worth about as much as a three-dollar pickle bottle? You feel that about all you're good for is to sit on a shelf? Take heart! You're worth far more than $44,100! God was willing to pay the death of

His only Son to redeem you. Not only that, but He has committed Himself to be available at all hours to listen to your prayers. He has promised never to leave you or forsake you. He is preparing a home for you for all eternity with Him. You're priceless! Never forget it!

Your heart may tell you something different. So will the world. And most of all, Satan will try to convince you that you're not worth much at all. After all, if you spend all your time being discouraged with yourself, you won't be as available to God for His use. Satan would love to foil God's plan for your life.

Neil Anderson has become well known for helping people deal with a damaged sense of their own worth. In his book *The Bondage Breaker*, he says,

> One of the most common attitudes I have discovered in Christians—even among pastors, Christian leaders, and their wives and children—is a deep-seated sense of self-deprecation. I've heard them say, "I'm not important, I'm not qualified, I'm no good." I'm amazed at how many Christians

are paralyzed in their witness and productivity by thoughts and feelings of inferiority and worthlessness. . . . Satan can do absolutely nothing to alter our position in Christ and our worth to God. But he can render us virtually inoperative if he can deceive us into listening to and believing his insidious lies accusing us of being of little value to God or other people.[2]

Don't listen to Satan's lies. God loves you so much, He gave His own Son for you. You are that valuable to Him.

That's it—the bottom line. Believe God's evaluation of you. Trust Him to accomplish His purpose in your life as you follow Him one day at a time. In a way, it's so simple, yet it is in direct opposition to the input you will get from nearly every "expert" around you.

Whom will you believe?

I press on to take hold of that for which Christ Jesus took hold of me.
PHILIPPIANS 3:12

The apostle Paul had plenty of bad things in his past. Before his conversion, he had been responsible for persecuting the new Christians; he was even there when Stephen was stoned to death. After his conversion, I'm sure Satan must have tried to keep Paul fixed on the past, wallowing in shame and regret over all the horrible things he had done. If Satan could have kept Paul living in the past, then Paul would never have gone on to be the great missionary who spread the Good News throughout the world.

Sometimes, though, we may *like* to live in the past, back when we were younger and prettier and stronger, when people we loved so much were still with us and needed us, when we felt competent and more in control of our lives. But God doesn't want us to live in the past anymore than He wanted Paul to. Whether the past was bad or good, God wants us to "press on."

God understands how weak we really are. In Psalm 103:14 we read that "He knows how we are formed, He remembers that we are dust." While challenging us in Matthew 5:48 to be mature or complete, "Be perfect, therefore, as your heavenly Father is perfect," He provides a way for us when we fall short: confession and forgiveness. "If we confess our sins, he is faithful and just and will forgive us our sins and purify us from all unrighteousness" (1 John 1:9).

Our goal in life should not be to pursue what the world says is valuable but to strive to be what God says is valuable. We should endeavor to take hold not of someone else's reason for being, but of God's purpose for us. I do not have to place a price tag on my value. God has already done that. My job is to "press toward the mark" of

God's purpose for me and to leave the rest to Him. Even if I appear to be a failure to the world I live in, I will trust His Word that "He who has begun a good work" in me "will perform it" until the day Jesus returns (Philippians 1:6).

1. Why does Satan want you to have poor self-esteem?

2. Have you ever experienced an identity crisis? If so, when? And why?

3. An identity crisis is not just for adolescence or midlife. It can overtake us whenever our lives change in some way, if we have been depending on something other than God for our self-worth. Are there major changes looming ahead of you in your life? If so, what are they? Do you think they will shake your sense of your own value? Are you at risk for an identity crisis? Why or why not?

4. Identity crises are never pleasant— but they can force us to realize that we have been depending on something other than God for our self-worth. Out of the pain, we can emerge with a stronger faith and a

true, biblical sense of our own worth. If you are not currently in the throes of an identity crisis, do you know someone who is? Pray for her today that she will use this painful time as an opportunity to grow in faith and grace.

Dear Jesus, I believe in You—and I want to find my value only in You. But You know how easy it is for me to get distracted. Before I know it, I'm depending on my talents or my natural abilities, my relationships and my possessions for my worth.

Lord, please remind me again and again that time will change all these things—but You will never change. When my identity is rooted in You, I don't have to fear the future. Thank You that You will always keep me safe. Thank You that You will love me no matter what.

AMEN

CHAPTER 6

BUT YOU DON'T KNOW HOW BAD I WAS!

Dealing with the Past

"I wish I could believe what you said tonight is really true," the lady commented to the minister at the close of the service. He had spoken of God's forgiveness, but the sadness in her eyes revealed that she had been unable to accept the truth of the message.

With tears filling her eyes, she added, "What I have done is so bad that I cannot ever forgive myself!" She felt justified in punishing herself for the rest of her life, willing to suffer the pain that guilt inflicted on her conscience, almost happy to be so miserable. She was probably thinking of the people who were hurt by her wrongdoing. Guilt hung like a millstone around her neck, robbing her of any joy that life might bring her way.

We have all done things we regret. We are sometimes thoughtless, hurtful, angry, or rebellious. We blurt out our feelings in a rush of anger, unable to keep the words to ourselves, and inflict pain on others. We act unwisely and put others in danger. We strike out, verbally or physically, and someone else suffers. Some of us have done truly horrible acts worthy of punishment but are never punished.

Then we realize what we have done. "If only I hadn't said that!" we say, or, "Why did I do that? I wish I could take it all back." Guilt rushes in when we realize that some words and actions can never be taken back, no matter how much we wish they could. The damage has been done, and we just have to suffer the consequences.

Even if those we have hurt forgive us, sometimes it seems impossible for us to forgive ourselves, and our lives are permanently marked by guilt, as with the woman above. When someone says she cannot forgive herself, she needs to understand two concepts.

1. Forgiving yourself is not the same thing as saying, "It's okay. What I did wasn't really so bad, after all." Sin, no matter who commits it, is wrong. It is an act

that affects ourselves and those around us. Ultimately, it is an act against God. We can never whitewash sin. All the rationalizing in the world can't change the fact that sin is wrong.

Many of us, though, have the idea that if I forgive someone (including myself), I must say, "What you did is all right. Let's just forget about it and not talk about it anymore." That is an incorrect concept. Forgiveness does not mean saying that wrong is right. Neither does it mean saying that the wrong didn't matter. It did matter. It hurt very much.

What forgiveness *does* mean is that when I forgive, I give up my right to hurt you (or myself) because you hurt me. The sinful act was wrong both in the sight of human beings and in the sight of God, but God has made possible a way of forgiveness that will settle the problem of sin. While it is wrong to commit sin, it is also wrong to continue to punish yourself for sin that God has forgiven. That leads to the second concept.

2. God will forgive you, and if He forgives you, who are you to refuse to forgive yourself? Remember, God is the Creator

of our entire reality. So if He says that you are no longer guilty, then that is what is real.

If you cling to your guilt, you are clinging to a ghost, a shadow of something that no longer exists. You may continue to be haunted by your guilt your whole life; this awful ghost may rule your life, keeping you from experiencing the joy God wants for you. But you don't have to live that way. God sent Jesus so that guilt would have no more power over you. Let the sunshine of His love drive away all the shadows and ghosts from your past. Don't cling to something that's now only an illusion. God's love and power and forgiveness are real.

Tracy was born when her parents were in their forties. When she was only four and one-half, her father died, leaving behind his wife and four children. Tracy was taken to church and given a foundation of faith that later turned out to be indestructible. Then her mother remarried, however, this time to an alcoholic. Tracy's home life changed drastically. Becoming bitter and resentful, Tracy blamed her parents and God for her unhappiness.

At sixteen, Tracy left home. She searched for love and an end to her inner pain through drugs, alcohol, and an illicit relationship. She was anorexic and suicidal. After a fight with her boyfriend, scared, hopeless, and alone—with a bottle of migraine pills in her hand—she took a desperate, drastic step. The next thing she knew, she was waking up to her stomach being pumped. Her roommate had found her in time. A week later, she discovered she was pregnant. When her boyfriend gave her the ultimatum, "It's me or the baby," she chose the baby, and in a few months the frightened teenager gave birth.

As a new mother, Tracy went back to church and read the Bible, but it was a shallow effort. She still carried the guilt and shame of her failures within her. She had not accepted God's complete forgiveness in her life. With her deep need to feel accepted, she went from one bad relationship to another. Then her life was ripped apart at the seams. She was raped—not by a stranger, but by someone she trusted. "I was so full of hurt, anger, shame, and guilt," recalls Tracy, "that I couldn't even pray for help.

The truth was, I was afraid to pray. I felt I was being punished for my life."

Tracy took her son and moved to another town, enrolled in a university, and got a job. A few months later she lost her job. With overdue bills and no money, she picked up food from an emergency center and returned home to find the gas shut off. It was the dead of winter and snowing. "I held my young son and cried," she said.

Then she made another irresponsible decision. She wanted a family for her son so badly that she jumped into marriage without considering that the man she was marrying was an alcoholic and drug abuser; she later learned he worked only to support his habit. To make things worse, she became pregnant again. The final straw came when her husband picked up her son from day care and took him with him to sell drugs. Tracy and her son left that night.

Tracy moved to California and two months later gave birth to her second son. Once again she found a job and went on with life. Soon after, she met Tim. By now she didn't trust anyone, but with kindness and patient perseverance, he won her heart, and they were married. Tim wasn't a real believer yet, and it wasn't until their daughter was born that Tim softened to the idea of going to church. They began to attend casually. Another surprise followed—Tracy was again pregnant, this time with twin girls. Soon they had five young children.

Tracy's life was better in some ways, but her troubles weren't over. Next she developed throat cancer and went through surgery and radiation. Six months later her oldest son nearly died from a very painful and never-diagnosed disease.

By now God had Tim and Tracy's undivided attention! When a friend invited them to Saddleback Valley Community church in Lake Forest, California, God used Tim's interest in music to draw them in. Now they have both committed their lives to Jesus Christ and are actively making their lives count for Him. Tim plays in the church orchestra, even though it means a long drive from where they live. Tracy is using her life experiences to counsel and teach pregnant teens.

"I have learned not to blame others for my pain but instead realize that it is my choices that put me in these positions; I am responsible. Now, forgiveness has come to my life!" One of her favorite verses is, "Praise be to. . .God. . .the Father of compassion and the God of all comfort, who comforts us in all our troubles, so that we can comfort those in any trouble with the comfort we ourselves have received from God" (2 Corinthians 1:3–4).

Tracy would tell you that no matter how deep into sin you have fallen, no matter how your life is scarred from the results of your choices, God is in the business of forgiveness and redemption.

In his book *The Mary Miracle*, Jack Hayford, a leading evangelical pastor and author, points out that in the ancient Roman world the word "Corinthian" meant "rotten to the core." The city of Corinth, located in what is present-day Greece, was known for its sin. In Paul's first letter to the Christians of Corinth, he lists some pretty bad characters: the sexually immoral, idolaters, male prostitutes, homosexual offenders, thieves, the greedy, drunkards, slanderers, and swindlers. He personalizes it when he adds, "And that is what some of you were."

But Paul goes on to declare, "But you were washed, you were sanctified, you were justified in the name of the Lord Jesus" (1 Corinthians 6:11). It would be wonderful enough to be washed, sanctified, and clean. But in his second letter to the Corinthians, Paul adds an even more astounding thought when he writes, "I am jealous for you with a godly jealousy. I promised you to one husband, to Christ, so that I might present you as a pure virgin to him" (2 Corinthians 11:2). Says Pastor Hayford,

> Do you hear that, dear one? A chaste virgin. Look at this awesome new creation statement in God's Word! See how former sin and sex addicts are now being declared "virginal!" Can you imagine a more towering statement on how vast the possibilities of God's restorative powers are, once He sets about recovering ruined, broken or sin-stained people?[1]

These truths are magnificent!

Matt and Jennifer were delighted when God sent two fine sons into their family, yet Jennifer longed for a daughter. In the back of her mind, however, she kept thinking that God would not give her a girl because of the life she had lived before she became a Christian. She believed that God wouldn't trust her to raise a daughter properly, so that's why He gave her boys. What a lie Satan was using to influence her image of God! Imagine her joy when the third child God sent to their home was a beautiful baby girl. Now Jennifer knew that "If anyone is in Christ, he [or she] is a new creation; the old has gone, the new has come!" (2 Corinthians 5:17).

This is where your part comes in. God has done the part we couldn't do—paid the price of forgiveness for sins. Now you must be willing not only to accept His forgiveness but to ignore the condemning thoughts that rear their ugly heads in your mind. You must say, "I know God has forgiven this sin, and so I must forgive myself and others."

This, of course, is easier said than done. Every person with some sensitivity feels guilt for their sins. Sometimes they tell themselves, "I couldn't forgive anyone who did that to me! How can I accept God's forgiveness when I've been so evil? It can't be that simple." Yet this same person can forgive the sins of others, even those that affect her personally. It may involve a bit of an emotional struggle, but most of us are basically forgiving people.

So why can't we forgive ourselves? Why do we punish ourselves for years over a mistake that God and the other people involved have long ago forgotten? This refusal to accept God's forgiveness and cleansing is almost a sin in itself. God has given you the greatest gift He could find, and we tell Him, "No, thanks. I don't believe I'm worthy of it, so please take it back." How would you feel if your child said that at Christmas? What if your mother-in-law said that when you handed her a birthday present? You wouldn't understand, would you? You'd think they had gone off their rockers, and you'd get angry. "My gift isn't good enough for you? Who do you think you are, anyway?" And you'd storm out the door.

No matter how we feel about God's forgiveness, no matter how unworthy we believe we are, if we refuse to accept His forgiveness and choose to listen to Satan, we hurt God deeply.

No sin is so bad that Christ's sacrifice does not atone for it. Do you believe this? Then resist Satan when he tries to haunt you with the ghosts of your old sins. Accept what God says is true about you. Ask God's Spirit to control your thinking, for "the mind controlled by the Spirit is life and peace" (Romans 8:6). Begin to live in the freedom of forgiveness.

Jesus came to our earth because we had all sinned. He came because of *you*. Nothing you have ever done could make Him ever forget about you. Amy Carmichael writes,

To me, one of the proofs that God's hand is behind and all throughout this marvelous book we know as the Bible is the way it continually touches upon this very fear in us— the fear that we are so insignificant as to be forgotten. That we are nothing. Unconsciously, His Word meets this fear, and answers it—not always by a direct statement, but often by giving a simple, loving little story.

John, looking through the thin veil of time into eternity, saw his Lord—the Lord he had seen pierced—now holding in His hand seven stars. John declares: "I fell at His feet as though dead." Immediately—just as though this fallen one mattered more than the seven stars, as though there were no stars—"He placed His right hand upon me" (Revelation 1:16–17).

Isn't it beautiful that there was no rebuke at all for their human weakness? And there never is a rebuke for our weaknesses either. "The soul of the wounded calls for help, and God does not regard it as foolish" (Job 24:12, Rotherham).[2]

You are important to God.

Guilt can be healthy. It can show us what needs to change in our lives. But God is offering you the gift of forgiveness through His Son Jesus Christ. All you have to do is reach out and take it.

Corrie ten Boom has a wonderful illustration about how to deal with the past:

> Guilt is a useful experience because it shows where things are wrong. It is dangerous when it is not there at all, just as the absence of pain when someone is ill can be dangerous.
>
> When we belong to Jesus we are not called to carry our guilt ourselves. God has laid on Jesus the sins of the whole world. What you have to do is to tell Him everything, confess your guilt and sin and repent, and then He will cleanse you and throw all your sins into the depths of the sea. Don't forget there is a sign that reads "No fishing allowed."[3]

A *Chain of Forgiveness*

Here's what I want you to do. Take your Bible and turn to 1 John 1:9. You may remember that we talked about this verse before. It's one of the most familiar verses dealing with sin and forgiveness: "If we confess our sins, he is faithful and just and will forgive us our sins and purify us from all unrighteousness."

Beside that verse in your Bible I want you to write a reference to Ephesians 1:7: "In him we have redemption through his blood, the forgiveness of sins, in accordance with the riches of God's grace." Now turn to Ephesians 1:7 and beside it write Psalm 130:4, which says, "But with you there is forgiveness; therefore you are feared."

Continue the chain of verses by writing next to that verse Psalm 103:12: "As far as the east is from the west, so far has he removed our transgressions from us." The next verse in the chain is Isaiah 43:25: "I, even I, am he who blots out your transgressions, for my own sake, and remembers your sins no more." Next to Isaiah 43:25 write Micah 7:19: "You will again have compassion on us; you will tread our sins underfoot and hurl all our iniquities into the depths of the sea."

Take time to jot down what each of those verses you listed in the Chain of Forgiveness says about the sin for which you have not forgiven yourself. Confess your sin to God and agree with Him that what you did was wrong. Then remember that it was for your sin that Jesus died on the cross. The good news is that you don't have to catch God in a good mood in order to be forgiven. In fact, I want you to understand that it is not merely because God loves you that He will forgive you. He has promised to forgive you based on the fact that His Son has already paid the penalty for that sin. You don't owe God for that sinful act. The price has been paid in advance, and you are debt-free once you confess the sin to God and accept His forgiveness.

Have you confessed your sin to Him? Has He forgiven you? The Bible says He will. Believe that He keeps His word, then resist the voice of Satan, who wants to accuse you of the sin for which God has forgiven you. The devil is called "the accuser of our brothers, who accuses them before our God day and night" (Revelation 12:10). The same verse says that someday he will be destroyed, but until then you must resist the devil's efforts to defeat you through accusations that are lies, not the truth.

"He [Satan] was a murderer from the beginning, not holding to the truth, for there is no truth in him. . . for he is a liar and the father of lies" (John 8:44).

"Submit yourselves, then, to God. Resist the devil, and he will flee from you. Come near to God and he will come near to you" (James 4:7–8).

"Be self-controlled and alert. Your enemy the devil prowls around like a roaring lion looking for someone to devour. Resist him, standing firm in the faith, because you know that your brothers throughout the world are undergoing the same kind of suffering" (1 Peter 5:8–9).

Let me suggest one more thing. Since it is Satan's job to try to get you to doubt God's Word, you probably should add one more verse to your Chain of Forgiveness, a verse that does not deal with forgiveness but with your thought life: "We demolish arguments and every pretension that sets itself up against the knowledge of God, and we take captive every thought to make it obedient to Christ" (2 Corinthians 10:5).

1. Before I can forgive myself or some-
    one else, I must first agree with God
    that the sin was wrong. If forgive-
    ness doesn't mean just saying,
    "That's all right, it doesn't matter,"
    what does it mean to really forgive
    someone (or yourself)?

2. Is forgiveness a fact or a feeling?
    Explain the difference.

3. What does it mean to you that in
    2 Corinthians 11:2 the apostle Paul
    says believers are "pure virgins"?

4. What does it mean for you to "take
    captive every thought to make it
    obedient to Christ" (2 Corinthians
    10:5)? Give a practical example
    relating to forgiveness.

Dear God, sometimes I can hardly believe that You can really love me. I can hide some of my sins and mistakes from others—but I can't hide them from You. You know everything I have ever done.

And yet, God, You love me. You loved me so much You sent Your Son to take away my sin. As hard as I try, I can never really comprehend Your love. I can never really grasp that from Your perspective, all the sins of my past don't even exist anymore.

No, I'll never understand Your love and forgiveness. All I can do is say thank You.

Amen

CHAPTER 7

*T*RASH OR TREASURE?

For Victims of Abuse

One of the biggest wounds to a woman's self-esteem can come from the sexual or physical abuse that was inflicted on her in the past. These wounds may go very deep; they may reach far back into a woman's childhood. As a result, this woman will be all too apt to have a deep-down, core belief that she is worth very little. Shame and self-hatred may be such an integral part of her personality that she thinks that's just the way things have to be.

If you are a victim of abuse, held captive by this sort of shame, I have good news for you: Jesus wants to set you free! What's more, He has the power to do it.

In his book *As Jesus Cared for Women*, Dr. W. David Hager talks about the woman who washed Christ's feet with her tears. (You can read the story for yourself in Luke 7.) Dr. Hager surmises that this woman had been wounded by men many times over in her life. She had been treated like an object so often, that she thought of herself that way, too. All her self-esteem had been killed.

How amazed she must have been when she met Jesus! Here was a Man who saw *her*— not an object. And He not only saw her, He loved her and forgave her. No wonder she cried as she poured perfume on Jesus' feet. "Perhaps she had cried herself to sleep on many lonely nights," writes Dr. Hager. "Maybe she had cried in pain when she was sexually misused by the men to whom she had sold her body. On this night, though, she was pouring out to Jesus a lifetime of pent-up guilt and anguish."[1]

Some of us have deeper scars than others —but we all have scars. Dr. Hager writes,

> When someone hurts us, abandons us, or embarrasses us, we decide that we will do whatever it takes never to let that happen again, making sub- conscious vows to guard the most vulnerable parts of ourselves.
>
> These vows may lead us to

behaviors that are evil or socially unacceptable before we experience forgiveness or that are self-protective even after we have come to know Christ's love. Yet, He is always ready to help us denounce those vows and to break down those walls that are really barriers to the inner healing God wants to do in our lives. He desires to care for our wounds, and He will, as we are willing to open ourselves to Him and to His loving ministry in our lives.[2]

As you read the stories in this chapter, remember—if you too have deep wounds from an abusive past, Jesus wants to heal those wounds. He loves you. You are more precious to Him than you could ever imagine.

There is no doubt about it: Kathy was a victim. The word dysfunctional hardly begins to describe her family. While her mom was pregnant with Kathy, her dad stabbed her in the stomach, trying to kill his unborn child. Her parents were teen-agers, both deaf and unemployed. A divorce soon followed, and Kathy and her mother went to live with her grandparents and two uncles who were only four and five years older than Kathy. The boys taunted Kathy endlessly, locking her out of the house, laughing at her cries for help—which her mother, being deaf, could not hear—and threatening her with violence if she "told" on them. Her grandmother ruled the household with an iron hand, giving orders for beatings to be carried out by an older uncle if she was not obeyed.

When she was about five, Kathy's young uncles began to make sexual advances, insisting she submit to their desires. Stopping at nothing in order to humiliate her, they didn't hesitate to beat her or burn her if she resisted. When more relatives moved into the small house, Kathy was forced to share a bed with one of these uncles.

Kathy enjoyed attending church and developed a love of God at an early age. She was still a child when her mother died after a series of strokes. After her mom's death, her grandmother condescended to let Kathy continue to live with her.

The family moved to another town and life improved for Kathy, but only for a short time. She was nine now, and because her grandmother was working again, she was required to do the washing, ironing, and cleaning, in addition to going to school. House cleaning included scrubbing the floorboards with a toothbrush and washing every wall, cupboard, and window each week—and woe be to her if she didn't do the job right! Once when a pot lid was not put on properly, her grandma flew into a rage, grabbed all the pots and pans, and threw them on the floor, along with the silverware, canned goods, plastic ware, cereal, and spices. Then she said, "I'm leaving. I expect this kitchen cleaned up spick-and-span or else you've had it when I return!"

Soon alcohol became a problem in the home. Grandma's parties often meant that Kathy was required to tend bar, dance, and, of course, clean up afterward. It was no better when her grandmother went out to bars, for then the boys had a heyday abusing Kathy. Sometimes when her grandmother had drinking debts, she would make deals with the men to whom she owed money and send Kathy to them. Depressed by the effects of alcohol, Kathy's grandmother attempted to drown herself in the toilet, threatened to kill herself with a butcher knife, and tried to jump from a car as it sped down the highway.

Because Kathy was a ward of the state, she had a social worker who visited her home about once a year. Kathy's grandmother turned on the charm during these visits, serving coffee and cookies, and being a gracious hostess. Kathy was too scared to talk. After her grandmother told the social worker what a fine girl Kathy was, the social worker would tell Kathy how lucky she was to have such a wonderful grandma with whom to live.

You may wonder why Kathy did not ask for help. Actually one of the priests to whom she went for confession questioned her about what was going on, but Kathy had been so beaten into submission that she blamed herself. She admitted some of the awful sins going on in her home—and the priest merely told her "not to do it again." Perhaps her self-esteem was so low that she simply accepted her lot in life as a doormat. Or she may have been ashamed to ask for help because she didn't want to admit the awful things she had experienced. She probably wondered if anyone would believe her.

By now Kathy did not care about school grades; she had joined a gang, used foul language, and knew how to shoplift. At the same time, she was becoming an excellent dancer. Her ballet teacher, Joyce, became an influence in her life; life at home was a nightmare, but life at Joyce's was

Kathy's ray of hope. She made excuses to spend more and more time at her teacher's home. When Kathy shared with Joyce just a little of what was going on, it was so terrible that Joyce was hesitant to believe her. But one day, because of bruises she saw on Kathy, Joyce asked permission to call her social worker. In addition, she invited Kathy to come live with her. For the first time, Kathy felt as if she had a choice, but she was torn. She loved Joyce—and strange as it may seem, she loved her grandmother, too.

After a fistfight with her uncles, Kathy made up her mind that she had taken the last blow she was willing to take, and she walked the fifteen miles to Joyce's home. It was a red-letter day for Kathy in more than one way, for on this day Joyce sat down with her and with an open Bible explained how to have a personal relationship with Jesus Christ. For the first time, Kathy heard a clear explanation of the gospel, and her heart ached for more. Joyce would not pray with her to accept Jesus that day, however. She wanted to be sure it was Kathy's own decision, not one made merely to please her.

The meeting that followed with the social worker resulted only in the social worker saying, "It's your word against your grandmother's, and they will never believe you." When her grandmother learned Kathy wanted to leave home and live with Joyce, and that she had told the social worker that her grandma had an alcohol problem, she went into a rage and began to slap Kathy and beat her mercilessly with a belt. "Jesus, help!" was all that Kathy could say, over and over. Then, Kathy says, a miracle occurred.

Grandma dropped the belt, began to cry, and said, "I can't hurt you. I love you, even though you've stabbed me in the heart."

For the next few weeks until Kathy actually left home, life was a nightmare of trying to placate her grandmother. One night during this time, her grandma was drinking extra heavily and was her old raging self, taking her anger out on Kathy.

"I went into Grandma's room and, sitting on the edge of her bed, I prayed a prayer like I never prayed before," Kathy told me. "Dear God," she said, "if I can know You like Joyce said and You care like Joyce said, I ask You to get me out of this house and let me live with Joyce. If You do, I'll give You my life."

"You are dead to me," her grandmother cried, "and I don't want to remember you ever again, and no one can even speak your name."

Kathy watched in horror as her grandmother ripped her baby pictures out of their frames and threw then on the floor at her feet. "You're not welcome here. Get out of my sight!"

Kathy said to me, "I told Grandma I loved her and said good-bye." There was no response.

"When I arrived at Joyce's she had baked me a cake." In addition, she had bought Kathy a bed and had it all made up for her. It was the beginning of a new life for Kathy.

When Kathy told me her story, I shook my head. "How could you function, Kathy, with a background like that? What gave you the courage to go on? Please don't glibly quote me 'All things work together for good.' I want to know how you kept going day after day."

"You asked that I not give 'spiritual' answers. Yet if I tell you what gets me through, that's all I have, for, you see, it is the Lord who gets me through. He is my Strength, my Sustainer, my Rock, and my Shield. I know I could never make it through without knowing who God is.

"I pored over Scripture," Kathy went on. "I read in 2 Peter that God has given us 'all things that pertain to life and godliness.'[3] With that Scripture I presented my petition to the

Lord and asked for help. I saw through Scripture that God is sovereign. He loves me unconditionally, totally, completely. God is love. You see, if I know God's character, it does not matter how I feel. Feelings are deceitful; they can't be trusted. When I felt like God didn't care, I knew that was a lie. Scripture tells me He cared deeply and tenderly for the lost, the crippled, the little children. Scripture also says He is 'the same yesterday and today and forever.'[4] So what I read in the Word was the truth; what I felt was a lie. That doesn't mean God doesn't care how I feel, but He also wants me to learn to trust Him."

"But, Kathy, what exactly do you do when feelings come over you that God doesn't care?" I asked her.

"I begin by saying the Scriptures. Sometimes I tell myself these truths a thousand times a day until I begin to believe them in my heart. I put them up all over the walls of my house, because I know the battle is fought in my mind: 'Trust in the Lord with all your heart, and lean not on your own understanding; in all your ways acknowledge Him, and He shall direct your paths.'[5] 'Casting all your care upon Him, for He cares for you.'[6] 'If you then, being evil, know how to give good gifts to your children, how much more will your Father who is in heaven give good things to those who ask Him!'[7] In Jeremiah the Lord asks, 'Is anything too hard for me?'[8] 'His arm is not short that He can't reach me, nor is His ear deaf that He cannot hear.'[9]

"Darlene, this is what gets me through."

"Okay, Kathy, I understand now that you've had a relationship with the Lord for a number of years and you know the Bible and God's promises. You know He will sustain you through these hard times. Your life proves that. But how did you know as a young girl that God was your answer?"

"At first I didn't," said Kathy. "My problems were too big for anyone, especially a little girl. I had to take a chance on God. When I prayed that prayer of desperation, 'God, if you let me live with Joyce, I will give You my life,' I only had God to turn to. Now I'm learning to fulfill my end of the deal. I offered my life, and what the Lord gave back is unbelievable—peace, comfort, understanding, joy, and always love. I would never trade my life with the Lord for anything, no matter how hard life gets or how difficult the circumstances are. Whatever I go through is nothing compared to what the Lord went through for me.

I love the Lord, and it's the love that constrains me to keep going, to put one foot in front of the other. If I get beat up along the way, it isn't any more than what Jesus went through. He is using my experiences to change me, mold me, and shape me, so I will be ready to spend eternity with Him. How can I complain about that? We need an eternal perspective."

Yes, Kathy was a victim. Nearly every one of the important people in her early life let her down. They treated her as trash. With a childhood like this, you would think that it would be impossible for her to realize her great value to God. Yet God is in the business of salvaging lives. Today Kathy is the wife of a pastor, a loving man who understands the damage that has been done in her past, and she is the mother of three boys. She understands and encourages other women who also are victims of abuse. Someday she says she'll write a book that she wants to title *Life Is Hard—But God Is Good!*

Recently my friend Ann shared with me about her struggles with bad feelings about her self-worth and value. She was raised in a home where she was constantly told, "You can't do anything right—you'll never make it!" These discouraging, defeating words took a strong hold on her life and outlook. Ann said, "Trying hard to win affirmation and to feel really good about myself, I tried all kinds of behavior, sincere and insincere."

Even after she had married a fine man and had two lovely daughters, a longing remained in her heart to feel worthwhile to herself and others. She sought help in a religion that taught her to think only positive thoughts, but that brought only further slavery, for now she had to prove herself in a different way—by being constantly positive. No one can be genuinely positive all the time, and so her religion forced her to once again deny her true self.

When Ann was in her thirties, a close friend introduced her to Jesus Christ. "She urged me to read the Bible and to open my heart to Him about my feelings. In my yearning to learn more about my Savior, I found the Bible verse that says, 'How great is the love the Father has lavished on us, that we should be called children of God! And that is what we are!' (1 John 3:1).

"This thought awakened my heart with a jolt! I realized I was the daughter of the Lord of lords and King of kings, His child forevermore. The change in my heart began. I was of real value to Him! I experienced a release from the bondage of having to prove myself and having to strive for self-esteem. I was chosen by God to bear fruit for Him. What an awesome privilege for my life."

Victory is never constant, Ann relates, but in those times of defeat, she repeats, "I am His child" each and every day. Restored again by His love and forgiveness, she can serve Him with a truly grateful heart. No longer looking for reinforcements to feed her self-esteem, she instead uses that energy to seek opportunities to glorify the Lord out of a heart secure in His love and in the joy of serving her Savior.

Ethel Waters once said, "God don't make no junk!" Maybe you feel like trash because the significant people in your life have told you that's what you are and have treated you like you belong in the city dump. Dear friend, don't believe it! Your database has been programmed with faulty information.

If you have been victimized in the past, study this book carefully. Look up each Scripture in your Bible and mark it. Then I urge you to find someone else who has also been a victim of abuse and begin to pray together on a regular basis as a means of encouragement. Instead of introspection or focusing on the past, go to work to lessen the miseries of others. Be open to help another woman who is struggling through experiences you have already had. As you begin to reach outward, you will be strengthened and encouraged in your own walk with the Lord.

If you are being victimized now in the present, please get help. You are God's child, and you do not deserve to live in fear. If you are married with children and have an abusive husband, you must protect yourself and your children by putting space between you and your abuser until he accepts help with his problem. And it is *his* problem. Don't believe him when he says it's all your fault and you deserve to be punished, because that's not true. You are a person of value, no matter what he tells you. Go to your pastor or find a shelter, friend, or relative who will take you in temporarily. Go to the police and ask for a restraining order. It won't be easy to do these things. After years of abuse, you will need enormous willpower to say "enough" and get the help you deserve, but with support, you can get out of the vicious cycle that is ruining your life and the lives of your children.

If you are a child still in school and feel you

are being abused, first talk to the uninvolved parent. If that doesn't stop the abuse, talk to your teacher, school nurse, principal, or pastor. Don't be embarrassed. This happens more often than you think, and people may already suspect something is wrong in your family.

You are not in this alone. The Holy Spirit will help if you call on Him, for He is the Comforter and Encourager. His work is to renew your mind and give you hope for the future. He can remind you of God's promises and "guide you into all truth" (John 16:13).

"One man's trash is another man's treasure," the old saying goes. I'd like to paraphrase that: "One man's trash is God's treasure!"

In Alma Kern's book *You Are Special*, she writes that

> Some of us were born to parents who wanted us and rejoiced at our birth. They received us joyfully as precious gifts from God. They raised us as best they could.
>
> Others seem to have been biological accidents, arriving unplanned, unexpected, unwelcomed, and unloved.

No matter what the circumstances of your birth, you are not just a happenstance of nature. God made you! God uses the best intentions of people. He can also overrule the worst intentions to accomplish His purpose.

You are special. God made you.[10]

He was despised and
rejected by men,
a man of sorrows,
and familiar with suffering.
Like one from whom men
hide their faces he was despised,
and we esteemed him not.
ISAIAH 53:3

If you have been rejected and abused by the people closest to you, you're not alone; Jesus understands your pain. He, too, knew what it was like to be rejected and hated; He knew how much it hurts to have people turn away and ignore your pain. He was the Son of God; He was there when the world was created; and He loved human beings so much that He came to earth to take away their sins. But the people He loved didn't want Him. Humanity rejected Him. They went even farther and tortured Him and spit on Him. In the end, they killed Him.

Sometimes when we're hurt, we look at the rest of the world, and it seems as though everyone else is happy and loved. We feel that no one else would understand our lives. But Jesus understands. We can pour out our pain and anguish to Him, for He has truly "been there." Ken Taylor paraphrases 2 Corinthians 5:21 saying, "For God took the sinless Christ and poured into Him our sins" (TLB). That's why Jesus faced rejection and pain: because He loved you so much.

The Gospel of Matthew, chapter 21, verse 42, says of Jesus:

> *The stone the builders rejected*
> *has become the cornerstone;*
> *the Lord has done this,*
> *and it is marvelous in our eyes.*

You too may have been rejected by people. The ones closest to you may have made you feel as though you are completely worthless. Your life is like a bunch of broken rubble, ready to be swept into the trash.

But God has other plans for you. He wants to put you in the beautiful mansion He is building. Jesus Christ, the same one from whom humanity turned away, is the cornerstone of that wonderful building—and He has a place for you too, a place only you can fill. You are not trash, but a precious stone, one of God's treasures.

Isaiah 54:11–12 says,

> *O afflicted city, lashed by storms*
> *   and not comforted,*
> *I will build you with stones of*
> *   turquoise,*
> *your foundations with sapphires.*
> *I will make your battlements of*
> *   rubies,*
> *your gates of sparkling jewels,*
> *and all your walls of precious*
> *   stones.*

When you look at your life now, you may see only smashed and broken bits lying in the mud. But God sees sapphires and rubies and sparkling jewels. Put your life in His hands—and one day you will shine.

1. What experiences in your life have
    made you feel like you are worthless?

2. Have you ever really dealt with
    these experiences? Or is it time you
    found someone to help you finally
    face them?

3. Our minds are like computers:
    When the same message is input
    over and over, we become pro-
    grammed to think the same
    thoughts over and over, until they
    become a part of who we are. If
    you have been the victim of some
    form of abuse, your mind has been
    programmed with lies that say you
    have no value, that you are unlov-
    able and worthless. You may need
    help reprogramming your mind;
    you may need to go to a counselor
    or pastor or a loving friend. But
    there is something you can do as
    well: You can begin to input new
    messages just as Kathy did, by

reading the Bible over and over.

Write down one of the verses from this chapter that speaks especially to you. Now read it over and over until you have memorized the main idea. You may want to copy it over on note cards and stick it around your house, in your car, in your purse. Whenever you catch yourself beginning to repeat that old, lying mental program, instantly turn to your verse. Read it over. Say it to yourself.

You will be inputting a new mental program, one of love and truth.

4. Pray for other women who have experienced the same pain you have. Ask God to give you opportunities to reach out and help. When pain is shared, it is always easier to bear.

5. Are you familiar with the Bill Gaither song that goes, ". . . All I had to offer Him was brokenness

and strife, But He made something beautiful of my life"? If you know it, try singing it to yourself whenever the past threatens to overwhelm you with bad memories. Remind yourself that God is making something beautiful and good out of your life.

God, You know all about the ways I've been hurt. When I felt so alone and unwanted, You were actually right there with me, grieving with me, hurting with me. You loved me from the very beginning. You chose me. I am not garbage.

Dear Lord, please heal me. I put myself in Your hands, all the scarred and broken pieces. Use me as You build Your kingdom. I want to shine for You.

AMEN

CHAPTER 8

*L*EARNING SELF-ESTEEM FROM JESUS

Following Christ's Example

I am sure we would all agree that Jesus was the most secure person who ever lived. John 13:1–3 shows us His strong sense of identity and self-esteem—and His utter humility.

> It was just before the Passover Feast. Jesus knew that the time had come for him to leave this world and go to the Father. Having loved his own who were in the world, he now showed them the full extent of his love. The evening meal was being served, and the devil had already prompted Judas Iscariot, son of Simon, to betray Jesus. Jesus knew

that the Father had put all things
under his power, and that he had
come from God and was returning
to God; so he got up from the meal,
took off his outer clothing, and
wrapped a towel around his waist.
After that, he poured water into a
basin and began to wash his disciples' feet, drying them with the
towel that was wrapped around him.

I was amazed when I first realized that the
answers to all four of those great questions of life
we discussed in an earlier chapter are answered
about Jesus in these few verses.

Jesus knew:

1. Who He was: the Father's Son,
    with power over all things (verse 3).
2. Where He came from: from God
    (verse 3).
3. Why He was here: to show human-
    ity the full extent of His love; to
    die (verse 1).
4. Where He was going: leaving this
    world to return to the Father (verses
    1 and 3).

Even though Jesus knew He was the Son of God, with power over all things, He washed His disciples' feet. Foot washing was the task of a servant, not a king—a mundane, stinky, messy job in the days of dirt roads and sandals. Even friends left this job to others, and Jesus was certainly more than a friend to His disciples. Still He chose to wash their feet, knowing exactly what that act would demonstrate to them.

Remember, at this time the disciples were all-too-human men. They often failed to live up to Jesus' expectations of them. Sometimes they doubted, other times they were afraid, and often they were downright stupid. In Mark 9:33–35 we are told that the disciples had a disagreement while walking along the road. While Jesus may not have heard everything they said, He heard enough to confront. "What were you arguing about on the road?" He asked them. "But they kept quiet because on the way they had argued about who was the greatest. Sitting down, Jesus called the Twelve and said, 'If anyone wants to be first, he must be the very last, and the servant of all.'"

In washing the feet of His disciples, Jesus demonstrated not only His own humility and willingness to come as a servant, but how He expected His disciples to live when He was gone from them. They were to live as humble servants, not earthly kings, willing to do the dirty work of life.

Jesus started around the table. He washed the feet of Peter, James, John, Thaddeus, Thomas. . . .But wash the feet of *Judas?* Didn't Jesus know that in a few short hours Judas would betray Him into the hands of His enemies and cause His death? Oh, yes, He knew! But Jesus came as the servant of all—even those who would kill Him. By His life and death, He offers cleansing to all—with no exceptions.

What does Jesus' example mean to us in our daily lives? Jesus did not boast about who He was—but how many times have we heard others describe, in great detail, their prestigious, high-paying jobs? Jesus never avoided a task that was beneath Him—but how many of us find an excuse not to volunteer in a soup kitchen or a free health clinic? Jesus never downgraded anyone else to make Himself appear better—while we constantly make mental comparisons between us and "them."

And we never read that all the while He was washing their feet Jesus kept reminding His disciples that He was the Son of God. He didn't say, "This is really not My job, you know." Or, "I hope you're impressed with how humble I am." No, He simply did the job, respectfully and lovingly.

A woman who is secure in her identity has this same true freedom to serve others in love. She can perform any task, no matter how humble, and still maintain self-confidence, because her sense of self-esteem is not dependent on her rank or position. The most recognized woman of our day, one who exemplified this attitude, was Mother Teresa. Willing to care for the filthy, dying poor of Calcutta, she displayed the self-esteem of one who didn't care what people thought of her, while caring a great deal about those to whom she ministered. I think we would agree that she was secure in who she was and what she was doing.

As we said in an earlier chapter, this sort of self-esteem has nothing to do with either pride or self-love. Instead, it is rooted in humility. "If you are humble," wrote Mother Teresa, "nothing will touch you, neither praise nor disgrace, because you know what you are."[1]

Jesus demonstrated this same humble self-esteem. If He could know who He was and who Judas was, and still wash the feet of the one who would soon betray Him, surely I should be able to find the grace and humility to minister to any fellow human being God brings across my path. Think about it. If Jesus could wash Judas's feet, can I say no if He asks me to do something good for a person I do not approve of? If I have the attitude of Jesus, I will be able to perform any task God asks of me. I can love any other human being without feeling threatened.

There's another side to pride that is sometimes even a greater temptation: putting ourselves down to others. A number of years ago an American family moved in next door to a Chinese woman. Wanting to be friendly, the Chinese lady made a plate of dumplings and took them to her new neighbor. As she gave them to her, the Chinese lady commented, "They're no good!" After the lady left, the American took her at her word and threw them out. A few weeks later the Chinese lady again took dumplings to her new neighbor with the comment, "They're no good!" Again the American threw them out, but this time her curiosity was aroused. After inquiry into Chinese culture, she learned that in old Chinese culture it was considered polite to discredit a gift when presenting it. Similarly, if someone should comment that you have a very fine son, the proper old

Chinese response was, "He is really very dumb!"

But when we do this in our culture, we're merely drawing attention to ourselves. Author Hannah Whitall Smith cautioned against this tendency: "Some people think they are humble and lowly in heart when they say bitter and disparaging things about themselves, but I am convinced that the giant ME is often quite as much exalted and puffed up by self-blame as by self-praise."[2]

A friend compliments you about the blouse you are wearing. What's your first reaction? "Oh, I got this for five dollars at a garage sale." When will we learn that a simple "thank you" is the best response? We tend to put ourselves down. Jesus never did that. He never denied who He was. He didn't boast about it, but neither did He ever deny it. He was secure in who He was.

No one can say Christ denied His divinity. On the other hand, none can say, "I am so low that He did not identify with me." Fully understanding who He was, Jesus did not act in an egotistical way, distancing Himself from people. He limited the expression of Himself while in no way denying His "personhood"—who He really was.

Can I do that? I think I can, to the degree to which I allow the Holy Spirit to control my decisions and my actions. To do so, I must have a clear sense of who I am—a person of value in God's sight—and a willingness to serve others, no matter how humble the task. I can follow in His footsteps.

Oh, I stub my toe a lot and wander off on side paths because I still want to do things my way. Every day I have to deal with my selfishness and with my tendency to argue about the details. "Wouldn't this other path be a little quicker?" I might say, or, "It's getting dark. Can't we go home yet?" I often get in my own way, and I sometimes lose sight of Jesus, Who is always walking ahead of me and showing me the path I need to take. But when I remember that Christ lives within me and that I can call on Him moment by moment for help, I come closer to His example. My nature fights hard against living this kind of life, because I am selfish, but as a believer I also have Christ living out His life within me.

That attitude puts self-esteem in its rightful place, in a biblical perspective. There is no room for either low self-esteem or egotism. I cannot say, "I'm no good—I will never accomplish anything important," because God has said I am a person of value. He has work for me to do for Him. Neither can I say, "I'm too important to lower myself to do that," because Jesus gave me an example by doing the lowliest of tasks for the lowliest of people.

What security! God loves me, and He has laid hold of my life for a reason. Day by day as I cooperate with Him, I can accomplish the purpose He has for my life, because I am a person of value to Him.

My oldest grandson and I have been reading a children's version of Charles Sheldon's classic book *In His Steps*. In the book the characters learn to preface everything they do and every decision they make with four words: "What would Jesus do?" Perhaps you have even seen someone wearing a tag with the message "WWJD?" on it as a reminder. Charles Sheldon's book asks,

> "Are we ready to make and live a
> new discipleship? Are we ready to
> reconsider our definition of a
> Christian? What is it to be a Chris-
> tian? It is to imitate Jesus. It is to
> do as He would do. It is to walk in
> His steps."[3]

Walking in Christ's footsteps is the path to true, biblical self-esteem.

Francois Fenelon was a man who lived in the seventeenth century—but he understood this same concept of Christ-like self-esteem. He wrote:

> Anxiety and misgiving proceed solely from love of self. The love of God accomplishes all things quietly and completely; it is not anxious or uncertain. The spirit of God rests continually in quietness. Perfect love casteth out fear. It is in forgetfulness of self that we find peace. Happy is he who yields himself completely, unconsciously, and finally to God. Listen to the inward whisper of His spirit and follow it—that is enough; but to listen one must be silent, and to follow one must yield.

What would Jesus do? That's a question that will guide us to a solid sense of self—a self-concept that's rooted in Christ.

*Your attitude should be
the same as that of Christ Jesus:
Who, being in very nature God,
did not consider equality with God
something to be grasped.*
PHILIPPIANS 2:5–6

Jesus neither boasted about nor put down who He was, either in His own thinking or His expression of Himself to others. He was God, and He knew it; He never denied His own nature or attributes. It is a false sense of humility (or is it actually pride?) that makes us think we must deny anything nice someone says about us.

Jesus was willing to come to us on our own level—without sin but with the limitations of humanity. In Philippians 2:7–8 Paul continues by telling us that Jesus "made himself nothing, taking the very nature of a servant, being made in human likeness. And being found in appearance as a man, he humbled himself and became obedient to death—even death on a cross!"

If I were setting those phrases to music, each would be in a lower tone than the previous one, but the intensity of each phrase would build, because each thought is even more amazing than the previous one.

Christ's work here on this earth was to bridge the gulf between divinity and sinful humanity. He Himself became that bridge. Although our task is not the same as Christ's, we are urged in Philippians 2:5 to have the same attitude Christ had toward His life work, namely to:

1. Know and accept who we are— sinners saved by grace and now accepted in Christ, justified, forgiven, adopted into His family, redeemed, cleansed, and in fellowship with God.
2. Be willing to identify with any other human being for whatever

purpose God may have for that relationship.

1 Corinthians 2:16 says that "we have the mind of Christ." When we follow Philippians 2:5, we will truly have the same "mind" as Jesus. His spirit of love and humility will control our lives.

1. In your own words, explain how putting yourself down all the time can really be just another form of selfishness.

2. Look at your life honestly. Are controlled by fear? Or love?

3. If you were totally secure in God's love, how would you live differently than you are today?

4. Is there some decision, big or small, that you've been struggling to make in your life? Ask yourself, What would Jesus do? If you're not sure of the answer, ask Him to show you.

5. A baby becomes secure in her parents' love by spending time all day long close to these people who love her so much. We too will become secure as we spend more time with God. Set aside some special time,

no matter how short, for being alone with God. And then go even further. Talk to Him throughout your day—at work, while you're driving, at home doing housework, wherever you are, whatever you are doing. He is always with you. Make a habit of including Him in your day. When you do, His love will begin to push your fear out the door of your heart.

Jesus, help me to have the same healthy self-esteem that You had when You lived on our earth. I don't want to be ruled by selfishness and fear anymore. I want to be ruled by Your love.

Thank You for Your perfect love. I give You permission to throw all the fear out of my heart. I want to be like You.

AMEN

CHAPTER 9

*T*OO BUSY WITH ME TO HAVE TIME FOR YOU

Self-Esteem or Self-Centeredness?

In her book *Keep a Quiet Heart*, Elisabeth Elliot says something that made me sit up and think. Writing about those who say we must unconditionally love ourselves, she first points out Jesus' words in Matthew 16:25 (Phillips): "If a man wants to follow in my footsteps he must give up all right to himself, take up his cross and follow me." In this verse are three conditions to being a true disciple of Christ: (1) give up all right to oneself; (2) take up a cross; and (3) follow our Lord.

Then she asks a disconcerting question: "Can we manage to juggle the building of a stronger self-image while we fulfill those three conditions of discipleship?"[1]

If anyone else had written that last sentence, I might have passed over the words. But this was written by a lady whose husband, along with four other men, was killed at the hands of the Ecuadorian Auca Indians while he was trying to reach them with the gospel. Moreover, his wife was left with a young daughter to raise. Not only was Elisabeth Elliot not bitter, however, but she continued working to reach these people for Christ and eventually saw many of them become believers; life grew from seed that had died, producing real and living fruit. Engraved in my memory is the picture I saw of her young daughter, Valerie, flying in a missionary airplane on the lap of one of the men—now a believer—who murdered her father. Elisabeth Elliot knows what it means to obey Jesus' call to discipleship!

I don't mind telling you, the idea of giving up all rights to myself makes me uncomfortable. After all, I have a good amount of self-esteem. I'm not about to lie down on the track of life and let someone drive the train over me. What does that get me? How is that useful to God? I want to protect myself, not offer myself up as a sacrifice. I want to feel better about me. I don't want to mentally erase myself from the chalkboard of life. I want to live. I don't want to die—and I certainly don't want to suffer.

Most of us are willing to acknowledge the importance of the cross in dealing with our sins. But what relation does the cross have to how we now live? Where does self-denial fit in with self-esteem? Author Ellyn Sanna discusses the difference between selfishness and self-esteem (what she calls self-actualization):

> Being selfish, however, is a very different thing from self-actualization (the process of becoming a real self). Remember the children's story, *The Velveteen Rabbit*? In order for the toy rabbit to become a real rabbit, he had to love and be loved—to the point of losing his original, plush identity. Only when he loved enough to be broken and hurt could he become real. And the same is true for [women]. We are not asked to deny our unique personhood, but like the Velveteen Rabbit—and like the saints—we are called to throw away our selfish

selves, so that we can become real in ways we have never been before, gaining a whole new identity.[2]

In other words, self-denial, the sort of self-denial that Christ lived, means that I am to deny all that is selfish in my life.

It does not mean that I am to go without proper food, rest, or recreation. I am expected to take care of myself. The woman who denies herself the things in life that she truly needs to function in a strong and healthy way is really selfishly keeping herself from being at her best for God, her family, and those around her. She is being self-destructive, not spiritual.

Self-denial has to do primarily with my will. It is a willingness to say yes to the Lordship of Jesus in my life, to do what He asks of me to the best of my ability, even if I have made other plans. God will not request more of me than I can handle. He knows my limits. I need to submit my life to God's leading, to be willing to step out in faith. That's not easy. Paul says I am to present myself a living sacrifice to God (Romans 12:1). But as someone else said, the problem with living sacrifices is that they keep crawling off the altar!

The only thing that works for me is to take my eyes off myself and put them on Jesus. If I am always looking inward, either to defend myself or to see if I'm really denying myself, I get nowhere. Then, as this chapter's title says, "I'm so busy with me that I have no time for you."

Remember that Jesus gave us three steps, not just one: deny myself, take up my cross, and follow Him. It's that third condition of discipleship that motivates me. When Jesus called His twelve disciples, He called them to follow Him. He didn't organize a committee meeting and draw up a contract for them to sign that outlined the job description and benefits package. He simply said, "Follow Me." What this involves is keeping my eyes on Him, walking where He leads, and obeying Him moment by moment.

I have no idea where that will lead me. Yet it isn't important for me to know the destination or even the path that I will be taking to get there; He whom I am following knows the way. My responsibility is simply to follow. That is the faith that is required to live the Christian life. "Trust and obey," as the old hymn says, "for there's no other way to be happy in Jesus, than to trust and obey."

The focus of my life, then, should be on

God and others, rather than on myself. Remember that in the two great commandments Jesus said I am to love God with all my heart, soul, strength, and might, and I am to love my neighbor as myself. That's a vertical relationship and a horizontal one.[3] What a contrast to our self-centered culture with its emphasis on me, me, me!

If I obey and follow God, will it cost me? Yes. Carrying a cross always costs. As Bonhoeffer put it, "When Christ calls a man, he bids him come and die." But in turn I know from experience that God is a good God and I can trust Him with all that is precious to me. I know, too, that the greatest satisfaction in life comes when I live God's way. Thousands of women have made that commitment and found that God is faithful.

You see, the self-denial Christ calls for is a self-denial with purpose, a self-denial that comes from love—love of God and love of others. Instead of focusing on myself, I am free to reach out to others. The apostle Paul put it this way, "Do nothing out of selfish ambition or vain conceit, but in humility consider others better than yourselves. Each of you should look not only to your own interests, but also to the interests of others" (Philippians 2:3–4). When I focus on God and others, I become relationship centered, which is totally in harmony with my feminine nature. I am free to nurture and build up the lives of people around me. I am free to meet their needs because I am secure in who I am. This is a real positive for women.

From the Book of Romans to the epistles of John, the New Testament is full of the phrase "one another." We are told to love one another, honor one another, serve one another, carry each other's burdens, be patient with one another, submit to one another, forgive one another, encourage one another, spur one another on toward love and good deeds, and offer hospitality to one another. The woman who understands her value in God's sight is set free from the need for continual introspection and therefore set free to reach out to others. As the Holy Spirit works in her life, she has the power and time and strength to minister to the needs around her. This is the life of true fulfillment. This is what biblical self-denial is all about: selflessness instead of selfishness, because I am secure in who I am.

Beth Albert was a missionary nurse first in the

Philippines and then in China, caring for lepers after World War II. Before she became a Christian, someone challenged her by asking, "Beth, you impress me as a person who is a hundred percent for anything you do; wouldn't you like to be a hundred percent for God?" Within days, she accepted the challenge and gave her heart and life to God, promising that she would be a hundred percent for Him.

Exactly six months later she heard about a leprosy mission that needed nurses. She completed her R.N. training, plus two years of Bible school. After spending time in Louisiana studying leprosy medicine and techniques, she left for overseas work.

She settled in Kunming, China. Here the governor had ordered that to eliminate leprosy the soldiers could shoot on sight anyone who appeared to have the disease. As a result, more than 120 people had gone about eight miles out of town to a cemetery, where they were allowed to live. They would sit by the highway and beg in order to survive. Day after day, Beth walked the eight miles to minister to these outcasts of society. She gathered rusting tin cans and taught the people, some of whom did not have fingers, to pack the cans with mud and bake them in the sun to make bricks. From these bricks, they built crude houses to live in. Even after the U.S. Consulate closed because the Communists were taking over China, Beth remained as long as possible to administer medicine and love.

Writing of her work, Bob Pierce, who was the founder of World Vision, said,

> This was the first time these lepers ever had anybody do anything for them. They were the most radiant bunch, and they all became Christians. They asked Beth, "Why are you doing this? Nobody ever did anything like this before." And she said, "Because I love Jesus and He loves you. He loves you so much He sent me to help you. You are precious to God and God knows you are beautiful. He knows you are valuable, He sent His Son to earth to die for you so that you might be saved and be in heaven with Him and be in a wonderful place and have a wonderful body. He sent me to show you that He loves you."[4]

Bob went on to say, "Beth was by all standards the most dauntless, ingenious, level-headed Christian I've ever met; and at the same time, she was the most joyful and the merriest."[5]

What do you think Beth Albert would have said about the terms used in today's women's literature, such as "cherish yourself," "make yourself happy," or "Isn't it time to please yourself?" Or how about this one: "Women are taught to sacrifice their needs for the good of those they care for and this depletes their self-love."[6]

God does not want you to *throw* yourself away because you think you are worthless. As we discussed in chapter 7, He does not want you to sacrifice yourself to an abusive or destructive relationship. But He does want you to *give* yourself away out of love. This sort of self-denial is rooted in true, Christ-like self-esteem. Because we know our value in God's eyes, we are set free from the trap of selfishness. We are freed to truly love.

God wants to use you in His service. Frances Ridley Havergal advises:

> Begin at once; before you venture
> away from this quiet moment, ask

your King to take you wholly into His service, and place all the hours of this day quite simply at His disposal, and ask Him to make and keep you ready to do just exactly what He appoints. Never mind about tomorrow; one day at a time is enough. Try it today, and see if it is not a day of strange, almost curious peace, so sweet that you will be only too thankful, when tomorrow comes, to ask Him to take it also—till it will become a blessed habit. . . .[7]

Let's make it a habit to make time for others. When we do, we will also be making time for God.

*And he [Jesus] died for all,
that those who live should
no longer live for themselves
but for him who died for them."*
2 CORINTHIANS 5:15

Most people live for themselves. They figure that if they don't take care of themselves, no one else will. "Number one" always comes first.

Jesus knew that this attitude is a destructive one. It's not only destructive to those around us, either—it's destructive to ourselves, too. It's that same old paradox that Jesus talked about in Matthew 10:39: "Whoever finds his life will lose it, and whoever loses his life for my sake will find it." The very thing we're trying so hard to protect—our own life—will be the thing we end up losing.

But Jesus died so that we could have our lives back again. He shows us the way to real life: a life that's built on love instead of selfishness. In the end, selfishness leads only to death. But love leads to life, both for ourselves and for those around us.

GOING FURTHER. . .

1. Personalize these phrases by writing
    down how they apply to your life
    in a practical way:

    Deny myself—
    Take up my cross—
    Follow Jesus—

2. How can you apply 2 Corinthians
    5:15 to your own lifestyle?

God, help me not to be "too busy with me" to have time for those You want my life to influence. Remind me to make a habit of taking time for others. I know that when I do, I'll really be taking time for You, too.

Show me today how to deny myself for You. Show me what it means in real and practical ways to take up my cross. And most of all, help me to follow You.

AMEN

CHAPTER 10

WHAT IF I FAIL?

Dealing with Perfectionism

In the first chapter I said I was not going to deal with specific problems that result from wrong thinking about ourselves. There just isn't space enough in one book to deal with all that. Yet I want to include one example so you can see how to apply the truth of God's Word to a particular situation. Perhaps this will give you guidance in a situation you are facing, either with yourself or a friend.

I have chosen the problem of perfectionism because all of us have a little of the perfectionist in us. Having been made in the image of God, we can conceive what perfection is, and we long for it. However, because of our sinful nature and selfish ways, we fail to attain it. In his book *Living with a Perfectionist*, Dr. David Stoop talks about the "aversion to the average that infiltrates every area of our lives."

We want the perfect marriage with the perfect partner. We also want to be perfect parents who raise perfect kids, who require nothing from us and do everything right. . . . Of course, that means we have to be perfect. We want perfect teeth, perfect skin, perfect weight, and perfect health. We dream of a family, a community, a country, and a world at peace—all in perfect harmony.[1]

If our self-esteem is not rooted in Christ, we feel that the only way we can prove our own worth is by being perfect. But if our sense of self-esteem depends on our being perfect, then we will always fall short. No matter how good we do, we will be frustrated and discouraged, because the truth is, none of us can be perfect at every aspect of our lives. We will sometimes let our husbands down; some days we will be impatient and selfish with our children; our houses will not always be clean and sparkling; and sooner or later, no matter how good we are at our jobs, we will make some obvious mistake that we can't excuse away. When these things happen, we are faced with the glaring truth:

None of us is perfect. Only God is, and we are all only human. But this need for perfection is the very reason many women struggle with a low concept of themselves.

In this chapter I am quoting from correspondence in my possession between a pastor's wife and her own daughter, who at the time of the correspondence was in her senior year in college. The daughter—Stephanie—struggled with this very issue: trying to maintain a sense of her personal value by being perfect. Stephanie was valedictorian in high school and graduated from college summa cum laude, but at the time of these letters she had just lost her straight "A" college average, and for a perfectionist, that is a tragedy. Read on.

Letter to Mom from Stephanie:

> Dear Mother,
> I am very unhappy with myself
> right now. I have ruined my GPA
> [grade point average]. I tried to put
> it aside but I'm so ashamed of
> myself. No matter how hard I try
> to pretend it didn't matter, I know
> it did. I didn't do my best and I

wish I were dead.

Mother, I don't know how to do it but I have to get rid of my terrible attitude toward myself and God or I don't think I can make it. I feel like He loves me but He wants everything I think is terrible just so I can become a better person. I feel like I'm begging God for everything and I don't believe He'll really give me what I want. I feel like everything I ever want is bad, and you know I want a lot all the time!

I hope you'll take this letter seriously and please try to help me. Please send me some advice and maybe a Bible study.

I love you so much,
Stephanie

Letter to Stephanie from Mom

Dear Stephanie,
I really appreciate your honesty in writing me and expressing your doubts and questions. You are right

—it is important that you find some answers to why you feel as you do. I can't give you all the answers, but I appreciate your giving me the privilege to point you in the direction where you can find answers yourself.

William Glasser, in *Reality Therapy*, says that we all have two basic needs: to love and be loved, and to feel worthwhile to ourselves and others.[2] I don't think you have any problems with the first part. You certainly know how to express love and you do express it in so many ways, and believe me, you are LOVED. But the second part has to do with how you FEEL— how you view yourself, and that's what's giving you trouble right now.

We tend to look for self-worth in two ways, Stephanie. First, how we see ourselves. We set goals for ourselves (such as getting a 4.0 average) and then we evaluate ourselves in light of how well we achieved those goals. Part of maturity is setting realistic goals for ourselves, and some of that comes only with age and experience.

The second way we evaluate our self-worth is through the reactions of those around us—how we think they see us. One of the reasons a girl wants a boyfriend is to reassure herself that she is lovable. But the basis of self-worth is first of all how GOD sees us. His opinion of us is an evaluation we can fall back on when we feel rejected by everyone else. (Have you ever felt no one really cared?)

Think about some of these things (maybe you can add more to the list):

1. I am unique—no one ever existed or ever will exist exactly like me; God brought me into existence at this precise time in history in a precise location; He knew about me before the world was even created.

    Ephesians 1:4 says, "For

he chose us in him before the creation of the world to be holy and blameless in his sight."

2. God sent Jesus, His Son, to die for me. (He could have zapped me and created a new person in my place.) Why did He bother? Because I have value to Him.

3. He didn't make me a robot but gave me a free will so I could choose Him and love Him; it's amazing that I can give something He wants to a God who needs nothing. He wants my love and praise of His goodness and greatness.

4. He says He LOVES me. Just read this verse: "But because of his great love for us, God, who is rich in mercy, made us alive with Christ even when we were dead in transgressions" (Ephesians 2:4–5).

5. My worth to Him is not based on my worthiness—how "good" or "perfect" I am. The apostle Paul asks, "After beginning with

the Spirit, are you now trying to attain your goal by human effort?" (Galatians 3:3). Also, I just noticed this week that in John 7 we read the Lord's Prayer, which says "Our Father"—obviously written to believers; yet, a few verses down in the chapter Jesus says, "If you, being evil. . . ." Obviously our God loves us for ourselves, not for how good we are.

Okay, if God loves us for what are and not for what we do, why bother trying to achieve and accomplish and do well? Here are some Scriptures you might want to look up:

Matthew 5:16—to bring glory to God

John 6:38—to follow Jesus' pattern: He did the Father's will, not His own

1 Corinthians 3:12–14—for rewards

Colossians 3:23–24—because we
serve Christ

1 Corinthians 15:58—because
what we do endures

Matthew 25:21—so that we may
receive His commendation, "Well
done, good and faithful servant"

So much for your attitude
toward yourself. You also say you
must get rid of your terrible attitude toward God—that He wants
everything you think is terrible just
so you can become better. Well,
first of all, check to make sure in
the back of your mind you're not
thinking that God willed for you to
make a "B." You must face up to
the fact that for whatever reasons,
you earned a "B," not an "A." God
didn't "earn" it for you. You know
the old saying, "I never promised
you a rose garden"? Well, God
never promised to shield you from
hard things—only that He would
never leave you or forsake you
(Hebrews 13:5).

John 16:33 says, "In me you may have peace. In this world you will have trouble. But take heart! I have overcome the world." My first reaction to that verse is, "If Christ has overcome the world, how come the world still gives me such trouble?" But the fact of the matter is that the last chapter hasn't been written yet. Someday it will be different. Because Jesus rose from the dead, He conquered death. The frustrating merry-go-round cycle of "Try, try again" will someday be over.

In this world we're not going to find perfection. That's why Paul talks in Romans 8:20–23 about futility and groaning and suffering. But our hope is Romans 8:18: ". . .our present sufferings are not worth comparing with the glory that will be revealed in us."

So far as the part about God wanting hard things in my life to make me better, remember that hard things come to *every*one.

You'll have them whether you choose God's will or your will. But the hardest things to bear are the ones we bring on ourselves when we choose our way instead of God's way. Remember Corrie ten Boom's tapestry with the mess of tangled threads? Yet on the other side the beautiful pattern can be seen. We may have to wait till we get to the other side before we see the whole pattern God is working in our lives.

One thing I've had to face in life is this: Romans 8:28 says, "And we know that in all things God works for the good of those who love him." ALL THINGS! Either it's true or it isn't—there's no middle ground. As you well know, when hard things happen you have two choices: either fight against them and get cut up and bruised, or accept them, asking, "What can I learn from this?" I do know that when you choose God's will, you have His promise in Psalm 91:14–16:

"Because he loves me," says the Lord, "I will rescue him; I will protect him, for he acknowledges my name. He will call upon me, and I will answer him; I will be with him in trouble, I will deliver him and honor him. With long life will I satisfy him and show him my salvation."

You said you feel like you're begging God for everything and don't believe He'll really give you what you want. Do you feel this way because:

1. God is not fair—He manipulates people; therefore, He is not good?
2. Because you don't deserve good things—you're not good enough?
3. Because you want some things outside His will?

My guess is you feel that way because of your desire for perfection —a perfect you, a perfect husband, etc., etc. Well, there just isn't any perfection in this life outside of Christ. But we do have some beautiful promises that God will give us the desires of our heart. Check out Psalm 37:4–5 and Proverbs 16:2–3.

You mentioned that you don't know how to love yourself unless you're perfect. I hope that's not our fault. I hope we didn't seem to withhold love when you were less than perfect, for we've always loved you so deeply and are so proud of you. Please forgive us if we did. Just make sure you don't make a god out of perfection. Ask yourself, whom am I trying to please? God? myself? my parents, or others?

It's tough to be the kid of highly motivated parents. I think this little story says it well. In a "Peanuts" comic strip, Charlie Brown had received his report card and was coming home from school. He was encountered by his friend Lucy, who immediately began questioning why he had not made the honor roll.

In the last picture, Charlie is alone, contemplating his lack of accomplishment, when he says, "There is no heavier burden than a great potential."

You have a great future ahead of you. The period of life you are in is one of finding out what are your abilities and disabilities, your strong points and your weak ones, your potential and your limitations. Be patient, "being confident of this, that he who began a good work in you will carry it on to completion until the day of Christ Jesus" (Philippians 1:6).

I love you so much!
Mom

Letter to Mom from Stephanie:

Dear Mom,
OK! You get the next hour until I go to lunch. I have been wanting to write this letter for a few weeks but somehow I hadn't been ready to go through the catharsis of it all.

Since I have returned this semester I have learned a lot! I feel like I have really changed. I now really believe that God has a definite, good plan for my life and I am confident that He will show it to me in time. I am concentrating on those verses in Jeremiah 29:11–13: "'For I know the plans I have for you,' declares the LORD, 'plans to prosper you and not to harm you, plans to give you hope and a future. Then you will call upon me and come and pray to me, and I will listen to you. You will seek me and find me when you seek me with all your heart.'" Now, whenever I think that things aren't going well, I just think about how much God loves me no matter what.

Last night I was reading Romans 5:8, which says, "God demonstrates his own love for us in this: While we were still sinners, Christ died for us." My imperfection is all part of the plan. Verses 2 and 3 of that chapter tell me I can exult in trials because I have HOPE! They say, "through whom we have gained access by faith into this grace in which we now stand. And we rejoice in the hope of the glory of God. Not only so, but we also rejoice in our sufferings, because we know that suffering produces perseverance."

I feel like the creation in Romans 8 ("subjected to frustration") because whether you know it or not, Mother, I really want to be perfect. Of course I realize I will not be until Jesus makes me that way in heaven. But someday I will be! In the meantime, I don't have to be!

If I already did everything right, God wouldn't even need His whole plan. He could have just kept His Son. I'm excited to think that my hope is God's love and it can never be taken away from me. And it doesn't depend on anything that is going on in my life. Maybe that is how Paul could be content in all situations.

I feel a lot more peaceful inside.

I think that as I realize these things and remind myself of them, as I grow, my acceptance of myself and everything I just hate will gradually become better.

I love you very much.
Stephanie

I wish you could meet Stephanie some day. You'd see a quite secure young woman who shakes her head in amazement that a not-quite-perfect grade point average gave her so much grief. "I think about those college years," she says. "I was in my own world—so self-absorbed." She says having a husband and two young sons has convinced her that "perfection" is neither possible nor important. She is looking forward to it in heaven, however!

Sometimes we all get discouraged—especially when our goals seem to be worthwhile, God-given ones. Hannah Hurnard, in her book *Walking Among the Unseen*, writes about these depressing feelings that strike a blow to our self-esteem.

I was growing very dissatisfied with

myself and my life. I meant so well and longed to be of use, but somehow I seemed to be so dreadfully powerless, so unable to help people in their sorrows, sufferings, and sicknesses as I longed to do, and as I believe we are all meant to be able to do.

I talked about this lack of power to the Lord.

"My child, what is your motive? . . ."

Whenever you react with praise and thanksgiving for an opportunity to grow more like Jesus in your way of reacting to things, instead of grumbling or feeling self-pity, you will find that the whole situation will be changed into a great big blessing.[3]

What are *your* motives? Your own success and perfection? Or God's glory? One will lead you sooner or later to frustration and discouragement. The other will lead you to a true, biblical self-esteem.

*We rejoice in the hope of
the glory of God.
Not only so,
but we also rejoice in our sufferings,
because we know that
suffering produces perseverance;
perseverance, character;
and character, hope.
And hope does not disappoint us,
because God has poured out his love
in our hearts by the Holy Spirit,
whom he has given us.*
ROMANS 5:2–5

The idea of rejoicing in sufferings seems pretty odd to the mindset of most people today. "Instead," as Scott Peck says in his book *The Road Less Traveled*, "they moan more or less incessantly, noisily or subtly, about the enormity of their problems, their burdens, and their difficulties as if life were generally easy, as if life *should* be easy." But, says Peck, the truth is, life poses an endless series of problems, life is always difficult and is full of pain as well as joy. . . . It is through the pain of confronting and resolving problems that we learn. As Benjamin Franklin said, "Those things that hurt, instruct." It is for this reason that wise people learn not to dread but actually to welcome problems and actually to welcome the pain of problems.[4]

This is exactly what the apostle Paul was saying in his epistle to the Romans. If we never ran into pain and frustration, difficulties and sorrows, we would never grow in our faith.

For those of us who are perfectionists (and many of us are, at least a little), this means that we have to accept the fact that life will never go smoothly and perfectly. But that's okay. God never intended it to. He knew it wouldn't be good for us if it did. If it did, then we could build our self-esteem on our own perfect lives instead of on Him.

Suffering, says Paul, teaches us perseverance. That means we learn to "stick with it." We don't give up easily; we just keep on plugging on. Just as water will eventually wear away stone, the ability to keep going in the end will accomplish great things.

William Carey, a nineteenth-century missionary to India, knew just how important perseverance is to God's kingdom. Year after year, in the face of failure after failure, Carey kept going—and eventually, he brought great changes to India as he spread the gospel there. He explained his life this way: "I can plod. That is my only genius. I can persevere in any definite pursuit. To this I owe everything."

Most of us think that great talents and perfect achievement would be more use to God. But through perseverance we learn hope, a hope that is firmly based in Jesus Christ. William Carey's motto was this: "Attempt great things for God, expect great things from God." He knew that his own efforts would always disappoint him—but his hope in God would never be disappointed.

Jesus never gave up either. As we follow Him, we will learn that our self-esteem need never be based on the apparent success or failure of our actions. By worldly standards, Jesus Himself was a failure, a man who died at thirty-three before His full potential could ever be realized. But God doesn't look at things the same way the world does. Out of apparent failures, He works miracles of love and life.

Here is Paul's prayer for the Thessalonian church:

May the Lord direct your hearts into God's love and Christ's perseverance.
2 THESSALONIANS 3:5

Let this be our prayer for ourselves also.

GOING FURTHER. . .

1. In what ways are you a perfectionist? In what areas of your life do you have the hardest time letting go of your goal of perfection?

2. Florence Littauer, in her book *Personality Plus,* says that some people are actually frustrated perfectionists. Because only perfection is good enough for these people, they've given up even trying. These are the people who may look like slobs and low-achievers. Do you see this tendency in yourself? In what ways?

3. As a woman, do you feel that the world expects perfection of you? In what areas?

4. How can you answer the world's demands for perfection?

5. Why is perseverance (the ability to keep on keeping on) more important than perfection?

6. List the four most important areas of your life. Now, with complete honesty, answer these questions for each area: Are you motivated to do well in this area so that you boost your own self-esteem? Or are you motivated by God's glory?

Dear Father, I'm involved in so many things at home, at church, and in my community—and all my responsibilities seem so important. I work so hard, trying to do all my jobs well, that sometimes I feel exhausted and drained. I want so badly to do everything well. If I'm honest, though, I have to confess that all too often I want to do a good job so that I'll look good to others, so I'll feel good about myself.

I'm forgetting about Your glory, aren't I, God? What a relief to simply let go of my need to do everything perfectly—and instead just do everything for You! You know I'll always make mistakes; You know that sometimes my best efforts will look like failures to everybody else. Thank You that I can simply relax and trust You to work everything out according to Your plan.

Help me to stop worrying so much about how I look to others, Lord. Remind me to just keep plugging, leaving everything else up to You.

And, God—thank You for loving me.

AMEN

A Final Word

WHERE DO I GO FROM HERE?

No, you may not always feel good about yourself—but you *can* feel right about yourself. You can know that you are a sinner, full of imperfections, gifted in some areas and limited in others. You may or may not appear to be "successful" the way the world rates success, but you are very valuable to God. He paid a great price to give you forgiveness and to allow you to have fellowship with Him through Christ's death on the cross.

If you struggle with your sense of identity, right here and now determine that you are going to do the following:

1. *I will accept Christ's death on the cross as sufficient payment for all my sins.* (God promised to forgive you if you confess your sins to Him. Make a conscious decision to trust His Word that the slate has been wiped clean.)

2. *I will forgive myself for the mistakes in my past.* (Remember that Satan is the one who continually brings forgiven sins to your mind. Recognize his attempts to defeat you by accusing you of a wrong for which God has forgiven you, and then resist him in God's strength.)

3. *I will accept my worth based on what God says about my value.* (Realize that overcoming old patterns takes time as well as determination. When you read your Bible, you build precept upon precept until God's promises become the foundation upon which you base your new life. Always keep in mind that you are a child of God, the daughter of the King [1 John 3:1].)

4. *I will settle accounts quickly with God.* (When you sin, immediately turn to Him. Admit the awfulness of your sin. Take responsibility for it. Then ask and accept the forgiveness He offers you. If you do this, you won't be burdened by a guilty conscience.)

5. *I will determine to lay hold of the*

purpose He has for my life. (You may not feel that God is using you for any lasting purpose, but decide by faith to trust His promise and wait for the results. That doesn't mean you will be exempt from problems or handicaps or even tragedy. Your suffering, however, will not be wasted but will be used by God for His eternal purpose.)

6. *I will refuse to let anyone make me feel inferior, just as I refuse to consider myself to be better than anyone else. By the grace of God I will be me!*

Remember, you are not a mistake; you are a potential masterpiece. As you put your life in God's hands and really trust Him, He will make you into the unique work of art that He has designed you to be. Only in eternity will you see and understand the completed picture created by God's workings in your life.

Most of all, never forget: Jesus loves you. You are infinitely precious to Him.

ABOUT THE AUTHOR

Darlene Sala lives in Mission Viejo, California, where she is active with her husband Harold in the ministry of Guidelines International Ministries, which they founded. Guidelines is a Christian outreach to 100 countries through radio, video, literature, and conferences. Darlene is an author, speaker, mother of three grown children, and grandmother of six.

For additional help, write to Darlene Sala:

IN THE UNITED STATES—
c/o Guidelines International Ministries
Box G
Laguna Hills, CA 92654

IN ASIA—
c/o Guidelines International Ministries
P.O. Box 4000
Makati City, MM, Philippines

NOTES

PREFACE

1. See chapter 10 for a sample application of these principles to a specific problem: "Dealing with Perfectionism."

2. Mary Hollingsworth, *Hugs for Women* (West Monroe, LA: Howard, 1998).

CHAPTER 1

1. Mary Hollingsworth, *Hugs for Women* (West Monroe, LA: Howard, 1998).

2. Karen O'Connor, *A Woman's Place Is in the Mall. . .and Other Lies* (Nashville: Thomas Nelson, 1995), 5–6.

3. Suggested reading: *Corrie ten Boom, The Hiding Place* (Washington Depot: Chosen, 1981).

4. Hannah Whitall Smith, *The Christian's Secret of a Happy Life* (Uhrichsville, OH: Barbour, 1985).

5. John R. W. Stott, "Am I supposed to love myself or hate myself?" *Christianity Today,* 20 April 1984: 26.

6. W. David Hager, *As Jesus Cared for Women* (Grand Rapids, MI: Fleming H. Revell, 1998), 87.

CHAPTER 2

1. Luci Swindoll, *You Bring the Confetti* (Dallas: Word, 1997).

2. Ruthe White, *A Spiritual Diary for Saints and Not-So-Saintly* (Irvine, CA: Harvest House, 1979).

CHAPTER 4

1. Joyce Brothers, "Men and Women—The Differences," *Woman's Day,* 9 Feb. 1982: 140.

2. Eugene H. Peterson, *The Message* (Colorado Springs: NavPress, 1993), 395.
3. Pastor and author of *The Purpose-Driven Church* (Grand Rapids: Zondervan, 1996).
4. Mary Hollingsworth, *Hugs for Women* (West Monroe, LA: Howard, 1998).

CHAPTER 5
1. Marabel Morgan, *Total Joy* (Old Tappan, NJ: Fleming H. Revell, 1976).
2. Neil T. Anderson, *The Bondage Breaker* (Eugene: Harvest House, 1990), 141.

CHAPTER 6
1. Jack W. Hayford, *The Mary Miracle* (Ventura: Regal, 1994), 99.
2. Amy Carmicheal, *You Are My Hiding Place* (Minneapolis, MN: Bethany House, 1991).
3. Corrie ten Boom, *Each New Day* (Grand Rapids, MI: Fleming H. Revell, 1977).

CHAPTER 7
1. W. David Hager, *As Jesus Cared for Women* (Grand Rapids, MI: Fleming H. Revell, 1998), 87.
2. Hager, 93.
3. 2 Peter 1:3 NKJV
4. Hebrews 13:8
5. Proverbs 3:5–6 NKJV
6. 1 Peter 5:7 NKJV
7. Matthew 7:11 NKJV
8. Jeremiah 32:27
9. See Isaiah 59:1
10. Alma Kern, *You Are Special* (St. Louis, MO: Lutheran Women's Missionary League, 1985).

CHAPTER 8
1. Quoted in *Women's Wisdom Through the Ages* (Wheaton, IL: Harold Shaw, 1994), 74.
2. Excerpt by Melvin E. Dieter and Hallie A. Dieter from *Hannah Whitall Smith, God Is Enough* (Hong Kong: Zondervan, 1994).
3. Charles M. Sheldon, *In His Steps* (Uhrichsville, OH: Barbour, 1984), 238.

CHAPTER 9
1. Elisabeth Elliot, *Keep a Quiet Heart* (Ann Arbor: Servant, 1995), 195.
2. Ellyn Sanna, *Motherhood: A Spiritual Journey* (Mahwah, NJ: Paulist Press, 1997), 16.
3. See Luke 10:27.
4. Franklin Graham with Jeanette W. Lockerbie, *Bob Pierce: This One Thing I Do* (Samaritan's Purse, 1983), 70–71.
5. From an abstract of "Charity Begins at Home," *Essence,* Oct. 1994: 73.
6. Graham with Lockerbie, 107.
7. Quoted in Mary W. Tileston, *Daily Strength for Daily Needs* (Uhrichsville, OH: Barbour, 1990).

CHAPTER 10
1. David A. Stoop, *Living with a Perfectionist* (Nashville: Thomas Nelson, 1987), 49.
2. William Glasser, *Reality Therapy* (New York: Harper & Row, 1965), 10.
3. Hannah Hurnard, *Walking Among the Unseen* (Wheaton, IL: Tyndale House, 1977).
4. M. Scott Peck, *The Road Less Traveled* (New York: Simon & Schuster, 1978), 16–17.

Inspirational Library

Beautiful purse/pocket-size editions of Christian classics bound in flexible leatherette. These books make thoughtful gifts for everyone on your list, including yourself!

When I'm on My Knees   The highly popular collection of devotional thoughts on prayer, especially for women.
Flexible Leatherette. $4.97

The Bible Promise Book   Over 1,000 promises from God's Word arranged by topic. What does God promise about matters like: Anger, Illness, Jealousy, Love, Money, Old Age, and Mercy? Find out in this book!
Flexible Leatherette. $4.97

Daily Wisdom for Women   A daily devotional for women seeking biblical wisdom to apply to their lives. Scripture taken from the New American Standard Version of the Bible.
Flexible Leatherette. $4.97

My Daily Prayer Journal   Each page is dated and features a Scripture verse and ample room for you to record your thoughts, prayers, and praises. One page for each day of the year.
Flexible Leatherette. $4.97

Available wherever books are sold.
Or order from:

Barbour Publishing, Inc.
P.O. Box 719
Uhrichsville, OH 44683
http://www.barbourbooks.com

If you order by mail, add $2.00 to your order for shipping.
Prices are subject to change without notice.